SYSTEM MANAGEMENT

SYSTEM MANAGEMENT

PLANNING AND CONTROL

H. W. LANFORD

National University Publications
KENNIKAT PRESS // 1981
Port Washington, N.Y. // London

Manufactured in the United States of America

Published by
Kennikat Press Corp.
Port Washington, N.Y. / London

Library of Congress Cataloging in Publication Data

Lanford, H. W.
    System management.

    (National university publications)
    Bibliography: p.
    Includes index.
    1. Management. 2. System analysis. 3. Bureaucracy.
I. Title.
    D31.L3155   658.4'032   79-28529
    ISBN 0-8046-9223-9

To Joyce and Mike and Ward

CONTENTS

PREFACE

The purpose of this book is to direct attention to a number of areas of vital importance to the system manager—areas largely overlooked or insufficiently emphasized in most discussions on system management. Although the literature on management is rich in the discussion of theory, I believe that John F. Mee's survey of those past historical concepts that have influenced managerial thought is of great assistance to the modern manager, particularly the system manager. By studying these concepts, we can understand why interest in scientific management appeared so late: how many modern ideas represent a complete reversal of earlier concepts; how valuable the dialectic process has been in the development of knowledge and theory; and how our own scientific and theoretical knowledge represents a series of incremental advances, building upon the hypotheses of earlier theorists and practitioners.

This book does not hesitate to present a defense of the bureaucratic organization, which in my opinion is the most effective administrative structure developed to date. Criticisms of the bureaucratic structure are examined, and in rebuttal it is pointed out that the alleged shortcomings of this form of organization can be remedied by improving the caliber of people who staff the operation.

Interface management and the management of conflict are explored. That interface management is a problem or potential problem is not usually recognized. The system manager, by determining the responsibility and accountability for each interface, can avoid many difficulties. The possibility—or indeed the probability—of conflict has only recently been openly discussed. Conflict was formerly believed to be symptomatic of poor management practices, but the likelihood of conflict under a large number of environmental conditions is now recognized. Armed with the knowledge that certain situations frequently result in conflict in individual and group behavior, the system manager is thereby better prepared to reduce their number.

Configuration management—another area of major importance to the system manager—is considered in some detail. Configuration-management procedures have developed rapidly in recent years, and with the consumer movement it seems highly likely that there will be an even greater emphasis placed upon them in the future.

The two primary functions of planning and control are of equal importance to the system manager—and to other types of managers as well—but perhaps of even greater importance to the former. As the vast amounts of resources placed under the authority of the system manager increase, wise planning and effective control become more and more imperative. With many system managers planning and controlling the activities of people who are in charge of spending billions of dollars—and most system managers are themselves responsible for the expenditure of millions—the effect on the national economy is obvious. Continuous research and lessons learned through practical experience have already contributed to the skills of the system manager. My hope is that this book will help to stimulate additional research into the many problems remaining.

The book itself is intended to serve as a supplementary reader for courses in general management, for courses in system engineering, and as a reference work for educators in management, for libraries, for management associations, and for use in executive training programs, company or organizational seminars and managerial development programs.

I am indebted to a great many individuals for assistance in completing this project, particularly to those system managers who took the time and effort to reply to extensive questionnaires on the subjects discussed in the text and to those who contributed through personal interviews.

I am grateful to Dean Richard J. Ward of the College of Business and Industry of Southeastern Massachusetts University for his suggestions about the organization of the book. The help of John Parke has been greatly appreciated. His suggestions served to improve many areas.

I am indebted to Air Chief Marshal Sir Frederick Rosier, G.C.B., C.B.E., D.S.O., presently Director, British Aircraft Company, for his review of the manuscript.

I would like to acknowledge appreciation to Group Captain John Calladine, Gloucestershire, England, for his efforts in my behalf. I am indebted to Professor B. Joe May of the School of Systems and Logistics, Air Force Institute of Technology, for ideas in the planning area, and to Thomas M. McCann, formerly Assistant Professor, School of Systems and

Logistics, Air Force Institute of Technology, and presently an established management consultant in Dayton, Ohio, for ideas in the control area. I appreciate the fact that Major General Gerald Cooke, Commander, United States Air Force Institute of Technology, took time to peruse the manuscript and comment on it.

Without the assistance of my wife, Joyce, the book could not have been completed. Her patience in proofreading each stage of the rewriting and her assistance in meeting typing requirements were truly outstanding.

I am indebted to the typists of the Wright State University Management Department for their steadfastness and diligence throughout a number of revisions, and to Mrs. Gladys Styron for her assistance in proofreading and typing the final draft. I alone am responsible for any errors that are to be found.

SYSTEM MANAGEMENT

H. W. Lanford (Ph.D., Ohio State University) is Professor of Management at Wright State University. He has developed and taught courses in system management, R. & D management, and technological forecasting, and has directed six technological forecasting/technology assessment conferences for the American Management Associations at both Chicago and New York centers.

While serving as an officer in the United States Air Force, he became system manager for a program requiring the expenditure of over eight hundred million dollars, and he also held staff positions in a systems acquisition division of the Air Force Systems Command which managed the expenditure of more than six billion dollars annually. He subsequently was director of the Electronics Production Resources Agency of the Department of Defense, and has been in consulting capacities for both military and civilian organizations.

Dr. Lanford is a senior member of the Institute of Electrical and Electronics Engineers, a member of the Academy of Management, the American Management Associations, and the Armed Forces Management Associations. He has been a guest lecturer for numerous educational and professional organizations and has contributed articles to national, international, and foreign professional journals. He is president of H. Lanford and Associates, Inc., management consultants, of Fairborn, Ohio.

He is the author of Technological Forecasting Methodologies: A Synthesis (1972), and coauthor, with B. C. Twiss, of Prevision Technologica Y Planificacion A Largo Plazo (1976).

1 ... TOWARD A WORKING PHILOSOPHY OF MANAGEMENT

INTRODUCTION

The aim of this chapter is to focus attention on the differences between system management and project management, terms sometimes used interchangeably in referring to the same organization. System management is the planning and control of group activities (some of the groups usually being outside the system manager's line of authority) to achieve with the resources available predetermined technical, managerial, social, political, and economic objectives. The system manager is also responsible and accountable for the management of whatever interorganizational and intraorganizational interfaces occur.

System management is characterized by activities and objectives having an identifiable life cycle, usually with a conceptual and development period of substantial length followed by the production and operational phases. System management accordingly requires substantial efforts to train personnel to assemble, test, maintain, and operate the end product, which may be either hardware or software—like the computer programs, for example.

System management generally requires extensive resources, both financially, and in the commitment of natural resources, time, and personnel. Although in the past, efforts in system management were usually directed at ambitious technical goals, it is anticipated that the same procedures will be applied as well to social goals on an ever-increasing scale.

Project management is usually associated with the techniques of matrix management—the short-term assignment of such specialists as engineers, scientists, and marketing experts to a given project, the specialists themselves remaining accountable to a supervisor elsewhere in the organization, who may occupy a position lateral to, senior to, or junior to that of the project manager. Project management may be defined as the planning and control—insofar as possible—of personnel and activities to achieve relatively short-term objectives with the resources available. A project manager is highly dependent on the caliber of the engineers and other experts assigned to the project, and on the ability, time, and dedication they are willing to devote to the project. A project manager is thus often required to display exceptional qualities of leadership.

System management, on the other hand, as we have already seen, is longer lived, has permanent employees, and has clear authority/ accountability relationships. It also supervises the expenditure of far greater funds and resources. Conflict in management, configuration management, interface management, the successful operation of the bureaucratic organization—these are all challenges to the system manager. Prior to considering them, however, it seems wise first to consider some of the directions of contempory management theory and some of the historical concepts that have dramatically influenced it.

MANAGEMENT FUNCTIONS

Many of the functions of management have been performed, perhaps often unconsciously, throughout the centuries of human presence on this planet. Earlier writers have invited attention to biblical allusions about the division of work and the number of subordinates that a manager can effectively supervise. In recent years researchers have also pointed out some identifiable schools or approaches to a theory of philosophy of management (Koontz, 1961). John Mee, in particular, has noted a number of stimulating historical concepts which have influenced society in the twentieth century, particularly that portion concerned with managerial functions.

Every modern manager needs to acquire a working philosophy of his or her own. Each manager must also find or develop an acceptable and comfortable definition or understanding of the functions of management and their implementation. In the ever-growing body of literature on the subject, there is a great deal of information, theory, and opinion on the identification, primacy, and relationship of management functions. The present discussion proposes to examine some of these definitions and correlations.

Figure 1.1 sets forth a framework showing the development of a managerial philosophy by separately considering the two primary functions of management—planning and control. Subordinate to those are coordination of thought and organizing—in the planning phase; and direction and coordination of action—in the control phase. Subsidiary again to the above and classified as tertiary are staffing, delegation of authority, responsibility, accountability, leadership, supervision, and motivation. All these concepts have been discussed, studied, and written about at great length by thinkers and researchers, both past and present, and their work can be divided into schools of thought indicating which factors they believe paramount.

FIG. 1.1: A CONCEPT OF MANAGEMENT

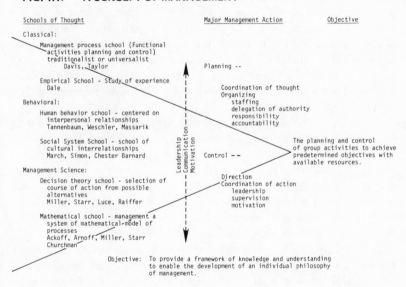

The aim of any study of management theory is the development of a working philosophy that will so facilitate the planning and control of group activities to achieve predetermined objectives with the resources available. (This goal is facilitated by the study of major management actions or functions.) These actions are categorized in Figure 1.1 to assist the system manager in the development of his or her own management philosophy.

The schools of thought shown in Figure 1.1 follow the categorization suggested by the now famous conference on management held at the University of California at Los Angeles in 1961 (Koontz, 1961). The emphasis or bias of the various social scientists and their work, is easily discerned, thus making it possible for an individual or group to assure that the management theory studied represents a well-rounded approach to the subject.

Most definitions of management emphasize the necessity of predetermined objectives, and further emphasize the organization of group activities toward the achievement of them. Some researchers maintain that management is getting things done through people; others, that management is getting people to do things. There is a not so subtle difference. One contribution of the behavioral school of thought is the demonstration of the long-term superiority of the latter approach.

Among management theorists and researchers there is a rather wide disparity of opinion concerning the primacy of various management functions. Ever since 1916, when Henri Fayol, the French industrialist, first advanced his concept of such functions, there have been agreement, diagreement, and modification. Fayol identified the following as the five functions of a manger: (1) to plan, (2) to organize, (3) to coordinate, (4) to control, and (5) to direct or command. As to the relative importance of these functions, it seems unlikely that any one best theory will soon be proposed or accepted. The following ideas and relationships, however, have served to assist system managers in the development of their own philosophy of management.

Let us define planning as those management actions that determine an acceptable course to achieve desired objectives with the resources available. This by itself is not too different from other definitions of planning. But note that the desired objectives are to be achieved "with the resources available." With insufficient resources, the objectives will not be attainable and will require modification in quality, time, or intensity. Here, too, is a convenient place to pause and consider whether the desired objectives have been stated in terms clear and understandable to all concerned, in a way that will permit measurement of progress toward achievement, and presented in such a way that the actions of management imply a dedication to achieve the objectives. In practice, it may be difficult to separate the management functions, but they can certainly be separated conceptually, and it is through conceptualization that we will analyze and discuss the various functions, and whether they be primary, secondary, or tertiary.

Earlier writers have listed steps in planning (Koontz and O'Donnell). The recognition of an economic opportunity or the need to solve a problem is given as the initial step in planning. The establishment of premises then becomes necessary. Technological forecasting, utilizing economic, political, and social-scenario inputs, is an excellent way, as we shall see, to establish premises.

Next is the determination of alternative courses of action to achieve the objective. The use of computers has made it possible to consider many more alternatives than was formerly feasible. Note that no attempt is made to determine the optimum course of action because "optimum" is too subjective an evaluation. The course of action to be selected should be the plan that is acceptable to the greatest number of persons involved in its implementation. It is far better to select a plan somewhat inferior technically that will receive wide support than to try to implement a technically superior plan that will cause resistance and not be enthusiastically supported by those responsible for its operation and success.

A proposal that some readers may find controversial is the concept of organizing as a subfunction of planning. To be realistic, a manager must organize around areas of expected results. The areas of expected results are themselves organized around effective supervisors, the most important asset an organization can possess.

As with so many other functions, organization is a circular process. The overall plan may call for a functional or a geographical organizational structure. Once the structure is determined, the supervisory positions are filled, from the top down, in a balance between selecting those having the qualities that senior management wants in each supervisor and those that are available. It may well be that the organization structure will be modified to take advantage of a particularly well-qualified supervisor or to accommodate a supervisory position in which all the desirable characteristics or traits are not found.

In the planning of the organization structure, and its subsequent staffing, the senior managers responsible for planning must implement the management concepts of authority and communication. The classification of communication as a tertiary function of management is a conceptual aid to the development of an overall working philosophy of management. Although important, communication cannot be perceived as being equally important with planning and control. Communication is inherent or pervasive in all management functions, primary or secondary, like leadership, motivation, concepts of authority, responsibility, accountability, and moral values—to name but a few. These all pervasive functions are, however, classified as tertiary for the sake of discussion, analysis, and understanding. By the same ground rules, the delegation of authority will also be classified as a tertiary function of management. The subject of authority and its delegation is so varied as to merit further discussion and clarification.

CONCEPTS OF AUTHORITY

There are at least four identifiable concepts of authority. Perhaps the most common one is that of formal authority where the source of authority is based upon the institution of private property—an economic concept—modified by social institutions, such as our concept of elected representatives in our federal Congress to make laws to govern our behavior. The Constitution of the United States guarantees the rights and defense of private property. In our society, we elect representatives to the Congress of the United States to whom we delegate the authority to propose and pass legislation, to approve the appointment of certain federal government officials not elected by popular vote, and to serve as a check and balance on the executive and judicial branches of the federal government. The members of Congress must approve the heads of the various departments in the Cabinet, who then delegate some of their authority to various levels of subordinates within their respective departments. Exercising our economic right of private property or ownership, those of us who are stockholders elect members of boards of directors of business organizations and delegate authority to them to act for us. Such boards of directors elect, appoint, and ratify the officers and senior managers of corporations. These officers or senior managers redelegate in turn some of their own delegated authority to subordinates on lower levels of management. This practice of delegation of authority (based on ownership) has found its way into organizations of a social nature in which membership is not based on private property—such as religious organizations.

There is also informal authority, which is that authority accruing to a member of a group by some means other than from formal delegation of authority. It may be bestowed by reasons of charisma, of age, of job performance, or of some specific accomplishment, such as in the realm of sports, for example.

What is known as the acceptance theory of authority is that concept whereby a subordinate in actuality determines the amount of authority he or she perceives, or permits, or accepts in a superior manager. This concept—in practice, a very valid one—means that any manager who has not earned the respect of subordinates will find his or her authority questioned and lack the needed ensuing level of support.

Functional authority—the fourth identifiable form of authority—is that which accrues to a person by virtue of superior performance in a given field of operation, this superior performance or expertise having earned the person the right to direct or advise other members in the group along operational lines.

Prior to the development of an organization, the senior managers or planners must understand the importance of these four concepts of authority and determine how much formal authority is to be delegated to those in certain supervisory positions and how much is to be earned. The ideal, but rare, situation occurs when the manager is the informal leader, is functionally superior, is charismatic, and subordinates accept without question his or her authority.

The importance of communication and its two-way nature should be clearly understood and planned in the organization and the organization chart. The perceived actions of senior management determine what the policies of the organization really are. The written policies are mere guides, whereas the actual implementation determines the character of the organization.

SCHOOLS OF MANAGEMENT THEORY

Twenty-five years ago, it was difficult for a serious student of management theory to recognize how he or she could embrace the philosophy of some writers and researchers in the field of management theory, and yet be unable to accept, because of on-the-job experience, or even fully to understand theories proposed by other recognized writers and researchers. The conference held at the University of California at Los Angeles in 1961 resulted, as we have already mentioned, in a number of observations concerning management theory (Koontz, 1961). It pointed out the cloud of semantics obscuring theories of management, a condition that had been worsening over the years. The fact that there are so many different meanings attached to the same words highlighted the necessity for the practicing system manager to select or develop a definition and understanding of each theoretical subject that was comfortable for him or her to put into practice, and to develop an understanding of the various functions that would add to the development of a working philosophy.

The word "coordination" is an outstanding example. Coordination has been described as being both the essence of management and all-pervasive in its functions. A lack of understanding of the word, subject, or function of coordination is at the root of many problems in practical management situations today (Lanford). Henri Fayol named coordination as one of the five functions of management, and the subject has since been studied in depth and reported upon by a number of authorities. Perhaps the most practical and understandable approach to the subject was presented by Ralph C. Davis in 1951, in which he traces the development of the meaning of coordination from Fayol's definition, "To coordinate means to unite and correlate all activities" through Alexander H. Church's, "A synthetical principle, it requires that all the divided units of effort, taken together, shall amount to the result desired exactly, i.e., without gap or overlap." He then combines these definitions with his own analysis.

Coordination, Davis states, consists of two sorts: the first is the function of developing and maintaining the proper relation of activities, either mental or physicial; the second is the "coordination of thought which has to do chiefly with achieving a meeting of minds concerning plans and their requirements. . . . The coordination of action has to do with relating the activities that enter into the execution of the plan." Thus, there are two types of coordinating activities that the system manager must take into account: (1) the coordination of thought, to be accomplished during the planning function, and (2) the coordination of action, to be accomplished during the control function. The rationality and practicality of this explanation are of great assistance to the system manager in understanding the problems of coordination and the implementing of planning and control procedures. There are too many instances where a newly hired manager slows the implementation of a previously made plan by questioning the wisdom of the original plan or disagreeing with it because of personal philosophy. The result is a breakdown of time schedules and as a corollary, increases in expenditures.

One result of the 1961 conference at Los Angeles was that six schools of management theory or patterns were identified. Later researchers have pointed out similarities in certain schools of theory, and thus reduced the number to three. These three major classifications are the classical school (composed of the traditionalist or management-process or functional school and the empirical school); the behavioral school (composed of the human behavior school and the social system school); and the management science school (composed of the decision theory school and the mathematical school). More recent writers have suggested adding the system approach or system management school.

Conceptually the classification of the various theories into schools has contributed significantly to the understanding of management theory and has assisted in the determination of just what management theory certain researchers and writers advocate. This classification scheme has contributed significantly to the development of an integrated theory of management by emphasizing or highlighting the doctrines that each particular school offers the manager. The theory that it now seems best to advocate is an overlay, if you will, of the tenets of the classical school, the tenets of the behavioral school, and the tenets of the management science school, with the skilled system manager applying whichever seems best adapted to the given situation.

VARIOUS SCHOOLS OF THOUGHT

The classical school combines the findings of the earliest, or first, school of management philosophy, set forth by Henri Fayol; the management process school; and the empirical school.

The management process school—sometimes called the functional school—holds that such management actions as planning and control can be identified and intellectually separated or divided for further analysis. This school also holds that these management functions are universal in nature; that is, that they are equally necessary in the public, private, and not-for-profit sectors, and that managerial skills are transferable from one sector to any other. The management process school holds that it is experience, reinforced by research, that provides the conceptualization, identification, definitions, and analysis or explanation of management functions. Equally important this school accepts important contributions from other schools and recommends their use. It also analyzes the management process, establishes a conceptual framework for it, identifies its basic functions and principles, and builds a theory of management from them (Koontz and O'Donnell).

Another view sees theory as a way of organizing experience (Dubin).

The empirical approach to management theory, by examining, through case studies, the practices of successful managers, establishes generalizations or principles from which guides to future action may be developed. The empirical school attempts to develop principles based on past successes to guide future action. In so doing, it appears to be very close to the management process school, but lacks the conceptual framework provided by the latter. The findings of this school, combined with those of the management process school, serve to reinforce the fact that the classical school is based on experience supported by research—a powerful combination.

The behavioral school combines the theories of the schools of human behavior and social system. The human behavior school is oriented toward the study of individual behavior in the work situation. Four fundamental concepts form the base for this approach: (1) common goals of individual and organization, (2) recognition of each person as an individual, (3) motivation so that each employee desires to achieve individual and organizational goals, and (4) a recognition of the dignity of each individual in the organization (Tannenbaum et al). The validity and wisdom of these concepts cannot be denied. These concepts should be in the kit of every system manager. Other areas of study and research by members of the human behavior school are motivation, morale, discipline, leadership, and the management of change.

Behavioral research done by this school has demonstrated how important in the achievement of motivation are the factors of recognition, understanding, and acceptance of given objectives. It has demonstrated how important the ability to empathize, or to see the situation through the eyes of another, is; it has demonstrated how important is the process of communication, or projecting a thought or idea to others with the same clarity with which the orginator sees it, with subordinates free to and encouraged to ask questions where necessary and to provide feedback. It has demonstrated how important is the task of integrating the interests of the individual with the interests of the organization, of the alignment of individual objectives with those of the organization. It has demonstrated the desirability of the development of team spirit to achieve organizational objectives.

Behavioral research has demonstrated how important in the development of morale is the quality or type of satisfaction with immediate supervision. This research has shown that the general morale is affected by each individual's overall satisfaction with his or her work situation—including compatibility with fellow employees, perceptions of the organization's purpose and objectives as acceptable and satisfactory, and that the organization is reasonably effective in the pursuit of its objectives. (Group job satisfaction is, of course, also influenced by the individual employee's satisfaction with pay, benefits, and working conditions, and by the general physical and mental health of the individual employee.)

Research has also demonstrated the importance of obtaining the individual employee's acceptance of the fact that the objectives of the organization are paramount. Employees must develop the necessary self-control to maintain organizational standards in the pursuit of organizational objectives, and personal objectives of individuals must be subordinate and willingly so. Research has highlighted the fact that resistance to change must be expected. Change threatens to upset the pattern of organizational and individual adjustment and is thereby perceived as threatening to the security of the individual. Once aware of this fact, the system manager can circumvent resistance by making sure that all those affected by the change understand the conditions that made it necessary and how the change will affect them personally. It is, of course, also recommended that those most affected by the change be involved in the plans for it. Research and experience likewise have made clear that the greater the speed of implementation, the greater the degree of resistance.

In summary, the human behavior school highlights many very important factors that the system manager should be conscious of in exercising his or her primary functions of planning and control. These factors are important to every manager, and equally pervasive throughout the primary functions of planning and control, as well as in the secondary functions of coordination of thought, organizing, coordination of action, and directing, along with those factors classified as tertiary—recognition, understanding, empathy, teamwork, morale, and job satisfaction.

The social system school or approach to management regards the society and the organization as forming a system of cultural interrelationships. As the name social system implies, it is based on sociological research. The social system approach recognizes both the formal and the informal type of organization. According to Chester I. Barnard, the formal organization is one with consciously coordinated activities, whereas the informal organization is structureless, its members being bound together by personal contacts, charisma of undeclared informal leadership, and common interests. Barnard found the functions of the informal organization to be (1) communication, (2) maintenance of cohesiveness in the formal organization through regulating the willingness to accept authority, (3) maintenance of the feeling of personal integrity, self-respect, and independent choice (Barnard, 1938).

An advocate of the acceptance concept of authority, Barnard viewed authority as involving two factors: First a subjective factor—the acceptance of a communication as authoritative; and second, an objective one—the charcter of the communication. He found an employee can and will accept a communication as authoritative only when the following four conditions are met simultaneously:

1. He or she can and does understand the communication.
2. He or she believes the communication is not inconsistent with the purposes of the organization.
3. He or she believes his or her decision to be compatible with his or her own personal interest.
4. He or she is mentally and physically able to comply.

This analysis is the basis for the belief of members of the social system approach that sanction for authority evolves from the bottom, that is, from the working employee—and flows upward through the whole organization, as evidenced by the willingness of the members of the organization to accept the authority of supervisors at each level.

The results of the research on this approach provide much food for thought. The fact that there are some members of society who conceive of authority in this way makes it mandatory for the system manager to be aware of this concept if he or she plans to utilize his or her knowledge to the maximum degree.

The social system school seems to have been based on what has been termed the Barnard-Simon theory of organizational equilibrium.[1] The organization-equilibrium theory is based on participation and motivation. The activities of a group of people become organized only to the extent that they permit their decisions and their behavior to be influenced by their participation in the organization (Simon). This theory describes the organization as a system in equilibrium, which receives contributions in the form of money or effort, and offers inducements in return for these contributions. These inducements include the organization goal itself, the conservation and growth of the organization itself, and incentives unrelated to either of these. The equilibrium of the organization is maintained by the controlling group, whose members may have various personal values of their own, but who have assumed the responsibility for maintaining the life of the organization. The social system approach emphasizes to the system manager the importance of communication, motivation, and the acceptance of authority.

The management science school encompasses the decision theory approach and the mathematical approach. The decision theory approach to management emphasizes the techniques of operations research for the consideration of alternatives and the selection of a course of action. Operations research is what Harold Koontz and Cyril O'Donnell have called "quantitative common sense." By this they mean emphasis on the scientific method of problem solving—the determination of facts through observation, the classification and analysis of these facts, the formulation of hypotheses concerning the relationships of the facts, tests to verify the hypotheses, and, if the tests do verify the hypotheses, the statement of the "principles" discovered and the use of these principles to explain past experience and to predict future results. Combined with the use of the scientific method is the use of quantitative data, the presence of predetermined goals and the determination of the optimum means of reaching the goal. This approach, through the utilization of statistics, probability, game theory, and programming, emphasizes the construction of a model, the investigation of alternatives, and the final selection of the optimum solution to a problem. It requires the statement of the problem, the assignment of probabilities to various outcomes, the assignment of a usefulness or value quotient to each outcome, and the selection of some criteria for decision making. Because both the objective and the

---

1.   Herbert A. Simon, a political scientist who has contributed significantly to management theory, credits the idea or concept of equilibrium to Chester Barnard in Barnard's earlier work *The Functions of the Executive* (1938). Simon himself develops this concept more extensively in his *Administrative Behavior* (1945), Chapter 6.

problem are stated, this approach handles complexities well. The relationships between various factors are put down on paper, and an attempt is made to avoid preconceptions and to eliminate emotion; the approach provides selective controls.

Although some prominent advocates of the decision theory school, as well as members of the mathematical school, aver that decision theory and the mathematical school were not intended to be, and never will be, a part of a theory of management, these two approaches have long been so considered as schools; and this treatment offers conceptual advantages, for both the decision theory approach and the mathematical approach offer many useful tools for the system manager. .

Decision theory, then, requires a formal statement of the problem for which various alternative solutions are subsequently developed. The manager next establishes an objective framework with which to determine the merits of possible alternatives by setting up a working empirical model and establishing relationships between relevant factors. Decision theory methods are thus available for the actual computation of the outcomes of various alternatives. This approach focuses attention on the problem, requires the identification of strategic factors, and aids in clarifying each part of the solution.

The mathematical school of management also evolved from operations research. This school takes a quantitative approach. Its advocates hold that all managerial actions can be classified under a single heading: problem solving. Proponents of this approach emphasize the need to establish a conceptual framework to consider the problem and the development of working models to establish relationships between factors. These quantitative models are classified in two ways: problem-solving models and optimum-value models. The ability to measure factors quantitatively is, of course, a prerequisite for the application of the mathematical approach.

Advocates of the mathematical school hold that the quantitative method is the only truly scientific method. The scientific method, of course, implies observation, hypothesizing, testing, and control; the mathematical approach defines management as problem solving. It is based on the premise that almost every managerial problem can be expressed in terms of some mathematical prototype and that by manipulating the model, management problems can be solved with mathematical accuracy.

The quantitative approach lays great stress on the evaluation of alternatives. The larger the number of alternatives considered, the greater will be the accuracy of the prediction. The greater the computational ease of the alternatives, the easier becomes the selection of the correct alternative. But the contribution of the quantitative approach is limited to planning.

It does not offer much assistance to the system manager in controlling the organization or in implementation of the selected method.

The experienced system manager is fully aware of the importance of the premises underlying the development of a model and of the importance of the relationships determined by it. To state it another way, one organization cannot use the model developed by another organization unless the managers of the second organization fully accept the premises and relationships developed by the first organization.

In addition to the three major schools of management theory so far discussed, some researchers have pointed out the desirability of adding a fourth approach: system management. Although no system management school of thought has yet developed, it does appear as a conceptual possibility, and there is more and more discussion of the system method. With reference to Figure 1.1., the question is, Should the system management approach be placed vertically through the other schools, or horizontally through the theoretical base of management thought as already portrayed by the three major schools of management? Any theory of system management must be developed in coordination with the theory developed to date, by a consideration of the conceptual functions of management—primary, secondary, and tertiary—and a dedicated pursuit of the objectives of the organization.

SEMINAL CONCEPTS IN CONTEMPORARY THOUGHT

Such management actions as the division of labor into areas of specialization, the number of subordinates to be effectively supervised, and the number of levels of supervision between the senior manager and the work force have been alluded to throughout antiquity. The discussion that follows is, for the most part, concerned with the period extending from the sixteenth century to the present.

Figure 1.2 gives the names of some of the writers who during that period influenced contemporary thought and shows the approximate dates when their seminal concepts began to have an impact upon society.[2]

---

2.   John F. Mee enumerated these concepts in his book *Management Thought in a Dynamic Economy* (New York University Press, 1963). The belief is that the tracing through time of these concepts does much to develop an understanding of the reasons why management theory has been relatively late in development and suggests some reasons that managers may have predispositions toward certain theories. Our society appears to be the product of what we experience and what we see practiced, rather than what we are taught is theoretically correct. What is theoretically correct is accordingly frequently disregarded because of prejudice. Then there is ever the instance of the manager doing as he or she is told to do, regardless of the morality or honesty of the action.

It depicts a time line, covering the years from 1500 to 2100, upon which are superimposed the various ages together with the writers and seminal concepts that contributed to social, political, and economic thought during this period.

FIG. 1.2:   MANAGEMENT THOUGHT SINCE 1850

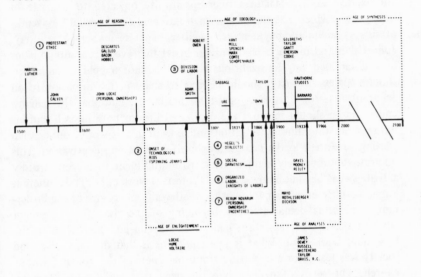

In Figure 1.2, the centuries from 1600 to 2100 are broken down into five major periods: the seventeenth century, which is known as the Age of Reason; the eighteenth century, known as the Age of Enlightenment; the nineteenth century, known as the Age of Ideology—with just cause for this was the period when many distinguished philosophers were formulating social and political philosophy, and early theorists and industrialists were beginning the development of managerial theory. The twentieth century is the Age of Analysis, again with good reason; and the twenty-first, the century of the future (2000-2100), is called the Age of Synthesis. The twenty-first century is expected to be the age of a comprehensive management theory, perhaps even the development of the hoped-for general system theory, providing all the scientific disciplines with a single integrated whole.

THE PROTESTANT WORK ETHIC

During the sixteenth century, Martin Luther—priest, biblical scholar, and linguist, who started the Protestant Reformation—and John Calvin—theologian, reformer, and ecclesiastical statesman—were the leaders of the movement that resulted in Western Christian belief being divided between the Roman Catholic and the Protestant views. In his protest against papal and clerical laxity, Martin Luther specifically objected to the sale of indulgences, which was the buying of forgiveness or of partial forgiveness of sins by monetary payment to specified papal agents, and to simony. John Calvin, on his part, espoused the belief that every man should labor in a disciplined and conscientious way in his chosen field of endeavor, should possess integrity, should be free to share in the initiation of an economic enterprise and to profit by his effort, and that through his endeavors he should improve the quality of life for both himself and his fellow man, thus finding salvation and reward in this world, rather than waiting to earn it in the next through self-sacrifice and deprivation. This doctrine—appropriately named after its commitment to diligent wordly activities—has become known as the Protestant work ethic. Today there is a marked difference of opinion as to whether the emergence of the Protestant work ethic demarcates the beginning of the rise of capitalism or whether the rise of capitalism had already begun and gave birth to the Protestant work ethic. What is relevant to us is that during that period society was ready for a departure from the tenets of the Roman Catholic church. The seeds of dissent—like the need for capitalistic endeavor—were present. For whatever reasons, the Protestant work ethic resulted in a radical departure from the religious, sociopolitical, and socioeconomic beliefs of earlier times. John Calvin, himself a Frenchman, successfully demonstrated the possible results of his doctrine by becoming the combined religious and civic leader of Geneva and enabling the citizens of Geneva to rise to positions of affluence through the production and trade of cloth goods.

In the seventeenth century, the Age of Reason, René Descartes, the father of modern philosophy; Galileo of Padua, one of the founders of the scientific method; Francis Bacon, philosopher and statesman; Thomas Hobbes, philosopher and political theorist; and Baruch Spinoza, philosopher and religious thinker, all thought and wrote. John Locke, who vigorously espoused the right to private property and who provided the basis for the defense of the doctrine of laissez-faire, was active at the end of this period. His contributions included ideas for the development of a new civil order that would possess (1) law based on reason, (2) government deriving its powers from the consent of those governed, (3) freedom to pursue individual goals as a natural right, and (4) the right to hold private property and to use it in the pursuit of happiness as a natural and legally protected right (Wren).

ONSET OF TECHNOLOGICAL AIDS

During the eighteenth century, the Age of Enlightenment, John Locke's work continued to have an impact on such figures as David Hume, philosopher, historian, and economist; Voltaire, social philosopher, moralist, and crusader against political and social tyranny; Adam Smith, political economist and philosopher; and Robert Owen, Welsh manufacturer and socioeconomic reformer. Although it may be argued that many mechanical labor-saving devices had been used earlier, the introduction of the spinning jenny is a reasonable point of origin for the second seminal concept, following the Protestant work ethic: the onset of technological aids.

DIVISION OF LABOR

The third seminal concept appeared shortly thereafter. It may reasonably be argued that division of labor had been practiced in earlier periods. Adam Smith, however, did perhaps more than any other individual to define and defend the concept. He pointed out how the individuals in a family production unit might increase the per person going rate of production from one to forty pins per day, when each worker performed all the tasks of pin making—bringing in the wire, cutting it to length, sharpening the point, forming the head, and preparing for shipment—to an unbelievable per person going rate of four thousand pins per day if the tasks were divided and each worker specialized in one given task. Division of labor and specialization had much to offer workers in a subsistence economy.

HEGEL'S DIALECTIC

Active during the nineteenth century, the Age of Ideology, were Wilhelm Friederich Hegel, the foremost philosopher of his day; John Stuart Mill, philosopher and political economist; Herbert Spencer, philosopher and evolutionist; Karl Marx, revolutionary sociologist and economist; Auguste Comte, philosopher and founder of sociology; Arthur Schopenhauer, philosopher and exponent of the metaphysical doctrine of the will; Charles Babbage, mathematician and inventor, whose work on the calculating machine foreshadowed the computer; Andrew Ure, chemist and professor, who was one of the earliest writers on the subject of manufacturing and production management; and Henry Robinson Towne, engineer and economist. It was in the nineteenth century that the four other seminal concepts appeared, the fourth being Hegel's dialectic. The dictionary definition of the term is "the art of critical examination into the truth of an opinion . . . logical disputation." Hegel's dialectic concerns the process of intellectual thought by which two opposites merge into a higher truth or synthesis—a unification of opposites. Hegel's dialectic proposes that all logical thought proceeds according to a pattern of thesis, antithesis, and synthesis. A thesis or premise or proposition is advanced which is immediately countered or disputed by its opposite or antithesis; this generates further thought and achieves a synthesis. Synthesis is, of course, quite disparate from analysis; it is a form of deducing reasoning that has to do with the assemblage of two opposite components into a single idea.

Hegel viewed society's development as a continuation of the dialectic process; that is, as one thesis is generated and countered by its antithesis, the resulting synthesis becomes in turn the thesis for yet another antithesis and synthesis. Karl Marx was influenced by Hegel's philosophy and wrote that social change must be accomplished not by writings, influence, and example as earlier social philosophers, such as Robert Owen, had advocated, but by abrupt, violent, revolutionary means. In brief, Hegel's dialectic holds that progress only occurs from the struggle between opposing forces or ideas and that the repeated swing from thesis to antithesis and back again results in a higher and richer synthesis.

SOCIAL DARWINISM

The fifth seminal concept is Social Darwinism. In 1859, Charles Darwin published his famous book *On the Origin of Species by Means of Natural Selection, or The Preservation of Favored Races in the Struggle for Life.* It was Herbert Spencer who substituted "survival of the fittest" for Darwin's own term "natural selection" and sought to apply to society, particularly to the unscrupulous members of the business community of the period, the principle of survival of the fittest that Darwin had demonstrated in his biological work. John Mee points out that "the belief that ruthless competition resulted in progress through the survival of the fittest led to practices that were not in the long run considered best for workers, small businessmen, or the public good." Fortunately, Social Darwinism is presently a less potent concept as society has seen fit to regulate practices of business organizations.

ORGANIZED LABOR

The sixth concept is the organization of labor, which brought about labor unions, and the concepts of collective bargaining and collective security. Although isolated attempts had been made earlier, in the latter part of the eighteenth century, with some degree of success, the particular date generally chosen for the beginning of organized labor is 1870, for it was around this time that the Knights of Labor, the forerunner of our modern labor organizations, started. From then on, the organization of labor continued steadily to develop, in spite of opposition by owners and management and such early disagreements about whether skilled and unskilled workers could belong to the same labor organization, whether labor's aim should be broad social reform or collective bargaining, and whether the organization of labor would ever be sanctioned by the federal government. It was not until the New Deal of President Franklin D. Roosevelt, however, that the recognition of the rights of labor to organize and to bargain collectively were firmly established through the passage of the National Labor Relations Act and the Wagner Act.

RERUM NOVARUM

The seventh and last concept is that of the natural right to personal ownership of property. The reader may recall that prior to the sixteenth century the right to hold private property did not exist. Property was held by the church and the state. During the latter part of the seventeenth century, John Locke, as we have seen, adovcated the right to own and protect private property. But it was not until 1891, that the Roman Catholic church recognized the right to own private property and provided an incentive to such ownership by publishing the *Rerum Novarum,* an encyclical letter of Pope Leo XIII. The *Rerum Novarum,* the first of the great social encyclicals of Pope Leo XIII, developed arguments establishing the natural right to the private ownership of property and setting forth the obligation of the state to protect that right.

THE DEVELOPMENT OF CONTEMPORARY MANAGEMENT THEORY

In considering these seven seminal concepts, we have attempted to demonstrate how changes in social philosophy and day-to-day practices have altered the outlook, expectation, and hopes of Western society, and more specifically of socioeconomic theory and management practices. Prior to the sixteenth century, humanity's earthly activities had been directed to the service of a feudal overlord, the church, and the state, with the hope for a better life in the next world, and with no entre-preneurial activities or opportunity for acquiring an estate to bequeath to one's progeny. Until then, the Roman Catholic church had been the major influence in the life of Christians. Martin Luther and John Calvin brought about the split in Christianity between Catholicism and Protestantism, and through the emergence of the Protestant work ethic gave men—no matter what their class—something to work for in this world. The seeds of capitalism were then sown.

The Age of Reason (1600-1700) developed many concepts with which to explain the political and socioeconomic world. John Locke, as we have seen, expounded a new civil order for man, with law to be based on reason—not edict; with the government deriving its powers, not through divine right, but from the consent of the governed; with the individual left free to pursue individual goals or objectives, not locked in indentured service to a master, the church, or the state; and the right to hold private property and to pursue individual happiness through the ownership and use of private property. These concepts marked a radical departure from earlier political theory, philosophy, and practice. They and the momentum that in the late nineteenth century the *Rerum Novarum* (1891) afforded, coupled with the results of behavioral research, provided the framework for the establishment of a philosophy of management, and did much to mold the value systems of contemporary managers.

The eighteenth century—1700-1800—the Age of Enlightenment, saw the onset of technological aids with the introduction of the spinning jenny, Adam Smith's *Wealth of Nations*, and the division and specializa-tion of labor. With the Age of Ideology—1800-1900—came the writings of Charles Babbage and Andrew Ure on manufacturing; Hegel and his dialectic, the concept of Social Darwinism, or unrestricted competition, and the survival of the fittest; the growth of organized labor for survival in the face of oppressive management practices—not yet entirely erased—and the strengthening of the personal ownership and private property incentive through the blessing of the Roman Catholic church in the *Rerum Novarum*. Henry Towne, whose works on the science of manage-ment appeared around 1886 and influenced Frederick W. Taylor, was one of the earliest writers on management to consider profit sharing by workers and the utilization of all resources. Towne recommended that the American Society of Mechanical Engineers, founded in 1880, become a focal point in the development of management theory. Frederick Taylor began his research in 1881 and published his first work on incentives in 1895.

The period 1900-2000 is called the Age of Analysis. Early writers in this century were Frederick Taylor, the father of scientific management (1900); Frank and Lillian Gilbreth (1900), early and prominent industrial engineers active in modern methods of time measurement; Henry L. Gantt, who developed the Gantt chart for scheduling work and following its progress (1901); Harrington Emerson, who formulated twelve general principles of efficiency (1910); Morris L. Cooke, noted for the improvement of productivity in municipal methods (1919); Ralph C. Davis, the brilliant management theorist who influenced a large number of present-day theorists (1951); James D. Mooney, best remembered for his analysis of the management of the Roman Catholic church and the principle of compulsory staff advice (1931); Allen Reiley, General Motors manager and author (1931); Elton Mayo, Harvard professor, psychologist, and sociologist, who, as a result of the behavioral studies undertaken in the early 1920s at the Hawthorne Works of the Western Electric Company in Chicago, theorized that workers behave like members of social groups and that work groups are highly important to worker behavior (1927); Fritz Roethlisberger, another Harvard professor also engaged in studies of human behavior at the Hawthorne plant (1927); W. J. Dickson, a third member of the Hawthorne studies team (1927); Rensis Likert of the Institute for Social Research at the University of Michigan, known for his research on employee-centered leadership (1947); Robert Tannenbaum, known for his leadership research (1961); and Chester I. Barnard, corporate executive turned author (1938). These are some of the theorists who have had an impact on the development of management theory in this century.

There are other important contemporary contributors, such as Warren Bennis, former president of the University of Cincinnati (1969), Professors Harold Koontz and the late Cyril O'Donnell of the University of California at Los Angeles (1964), well known for their direction of the conference in 1961 that resulted in identifiable schools of management thought, and others comprising a list too long to enumerate. William James, philosopher and psychologist, leader of the philosophical movement of pragmatism (1890); John Dewey, philosopher and educator, one of the founders of the progressive school of education (1884); Bertrand Russell, an outstanding figure in twentieth-century mathematics and philosophy, known for his work in mathematical logic (1913); and Alfred North Whitehead, mathematician and philosopher who developed a comprehensive metaphysical theory (1913), have also influenced the thinking in our century. The Hawthorne studies, mentioned earlier, are often regarded as the birth of the behavioralist emphasis.

The traditional school of management theory, incorporating the techniques furnished by the behavioralists and management scientists, appears to offer an approach to a central theory of management. The value system of individual managers is an evolutionary process. Research seeks ways to understand value perceptions, to improve the indoctrination of managers, and to raise the level of value systems to an even higher plane. Society's concepts of various subjects have changed through the years. The pendulum of thought swings both widely and slowly.

A UNIFIED THEORY OF MANAGEMENT?

The future century of 2000-2100 has been called the Age of Synthesis. During this century, it is expected that managers and philosophers will synthesize or put together the tenets of the traditional school, the empirical school, the behavioral school, the social system school, the decisions theory school, the mathematical school, the system management and whatever other schools of management theory develop between now and then into one acceptable central theory of management.

The synthesis or resolution of antithetical views continues to develop socially beneficial philosophical concepts. It should be a continuing objective of management theorists and practitioners to synthesize the valuable results of research so far achieved in the management area into a viable and acceptable unified theory of management.

THE EFFECTIVE ADMINISTRATOR

Regardless of the school of theory embraced, management theorists and practitioners are now aware of the many complexities facing management. It is recognized that a successful manager and effective administrator must possess three basic skills: (1) technical, (2) human, and (3) conceptual (Katz).

The effective administrator also must have sufficient technical skill to perform the mechanics of the particular job for which he is responsible; sufficient human skill in working with others to be an effective group leader and to be able to build cooperative effort within the team he or she leads; and sufficient conceptual skill to recognize the interrelationships of the various factors involved in the situation, which will lead him or her to take whatever action is most likely to benefit the entire organization.

2 ... THE BUREAUCRATIC ORGANIZATION

INTRODUCTION

The bureaucratic organization has been so widely criticized that the very word "bureaucratic" now connotes something undesirable, something unsatisfactory, perhaps even unsavory in the minds of many. This chapter provides a defense of the bureaucratic organization and makes the rather pointed suggestion that it is the managers and subordinates who staff the organization who are at fault, rather than the hierarchical structure.

Throughout history human beings have understood the need for organization to get tasks accomplished by groups of people. The principles of organization are alluded to in the Bible—"overseer of ten, of fifty, of one hundred," for example—and various forms of organization have been used, ranging from slavery and the feudal system of early history to the so-called democratic organizational plan—endorsed by some prominent theorists—in which management by consensus is attempted.

THE BUREAUCRATIC ORGANIZATION DEFINED

The type of organization designed to accomplish large-scale administrative tasks by systematically coordinating the work of many individuals is called a bureaucracy (Blau). Its basic characteristics are specialization, a hierarchy of authority, a system of rules, and impersonal authority. Impersonal authority creates the detachment necessary to make administrative decisions on the basis of efficiency.

It must be emphasized that the whole purpose of a bureaucratic organization is to achieve the objectives with efficiency, not to provide an opportunity for all participants or members to voice an opinion on the desirability or method of attainment of an objective.

CRITICISMS AND REBUTTAL

The fact that some organizations, such as some political parties, business corporations, and labor unions, have transferred powers that rightly belong to their members or stockholders to these organizations' management does not mean that such a practice is inherent in the bureaucratic form of organization, but a threat to and misuse of democratic rights. A bureaucracy is not necessarily antidemocratic; the character of any bureaucratic organization is determined by the character of its management. The democratic government we enjoy is based on a set of checks and balances. Just as our government has regulatory agencies, so must the bureaucratic organization—or any other type of organization—also employ a system of checks and balances. No system of checks and balances is an automatic part of an organization; it must be built in. Although the greatest safeguard is integrity of management, policies, procedures, and regulations, an independent internal auditing agency and a realistic channel for appeal are still necessary. It is easy to see that an appointed deliberative body, such as a board composed of puppets, is not a manifestation of democratic organization. A bureaucratic organization can, of course, be a democratic organization. But—to reiterate —it is the people who manage the organization that determine its character rather than the character being determined by the structure.

Warren G. Bennis, formerly president of the University of Cincinnati and an outstanding behavioral scientist, who has perhaps done as much study of the bureaucratic organization as any other researcher, has made the following criticisms of bureaucracy (Bennis, 1966a):

1. Bureaucracy does not allow for personal growth and development.
2. It develops conformity.
3. It overlooks the informal organization—those groups of employees brought together by common interests, desire for security, need for status, or just friendships—that exist within the formal organization. The informal groups serve as communication channels, social groups, and sources of influence—and, to some degree, as a balance against the formal organization.
4. Its system of control and concept of authority are outdated.

5. It has no inherent, built-in, independent channel or process of appeal.

6. It does not provide means to adjudicate professional disagreements (and jealousies) between professional groups or specializations—e.g., differences between engineers versus accountants.

7. Its hierarchy inhibits two-way communication and the flow of innovative ideas.

8. Lack of integrity in senior management prevents full use of the best human resources.

9. It cannot assimilate the influx of new technology or scientists.

10. It molds human resources into "the organization man."

The reader is now invited to consider each of these criticisms separately and decide whether the criticism is aimed at the bureaucratic organization or at human behavior.

Concerning the lack of opportunity for personal growth and development, the reader is asked to consider the example of Dwight D. Eisenhower —first, Lieutenant Eisenhower; later, General Eisenhower; and eventually President Eisenhower. President Eisenhower was a product of the United States Army, an outstanding example of a bureaucratic organization. Examples of other outstanding leaders who developed in government or private sector bureaucratic organizations are commonplace.

A look at the achievements of America's industrial leaders and the record they have amassed in developing new inventions, new processes, new materials, and new products is sufficient rebuttal to the allegation that the bureaucratic organization develops conformity and group-think. There is no argument about the fact that some people are reluctant—even afraid—to question the status quo or to suggest improved ways to do things. Students of human behavior believe that a person's personality and character are shaped very early in life, before affiliation with any organization except the family. It is unrealistic to place the blame for individual shortcomings on any type of formal organization.

Much can be said about the relationship of the formal to the informal organization. It is the formal hierarchical organization that is responsible for the research that brought about the understanding of the informal organization. And the formal organization can therefore be thanked for the resultant implementation of the recommendations of that research. But, when we stop to think, is this actually a true statement? Should we not rather thank the managers—the people—in the formal organization for implementing the recommendations of the research that resulted in the recognition of the existence of the informal organization?

Theories about authority are continually being improved and were significantly improved in the last generation. Theories in the social sciences continue to improve incrementally, as do theories in the physical sciences. Methods of control continue to improve—note the quantum improvement that PERT (Program Evaluation and Review Technique) offered the last generation and the promises that the work-breakdown structure offer this one.

If an organization has no adjudicative process of appeal, it would seem nowadays that most of the personnel of the organization does not *want* an appeal process to hear complaints. It is true that the existence of an appeal board does not guarantee the administration of justice, due to the danger that such a board may by design be composed of puppets. The very existence of labor unions and such professional organizations as the AAUP (American Association of University Professors) and the IEEE (Institute of Electrical and Electronics Engineers), however, has done much to insure the practice of integrity in senior management. Admittedly, if senior management is not committed to ethical practices, the establishment and administration of a fair juridical process is difficult, though not impossible.

Such agencies as inside and outside auditors and boards of inspectors are designed to provide a juridical process, and, where allowed or encouraged, do a good job of seeing that every member of an organization performs in accordance with its prescribed policies, procedures, and instructions. Of course, there is always the possibility that either an incompetent or a crony of the manager possessing low moral fiber will be appointed to head an audit-type agency, rendering it ineffective by design. The point is that the framework for a guardian agency exists in the bureaucratic organization. Once again, whether such an agency is effective is dependent upon the human behavior of those both inside and outside the agency.

As human beings, we jealously guard what we consider to be our own domain and prerogatives. We tend to take a parochial view of others' contributions and the division of recognition and rewards. All too often we are reluctant to share the credit for the achievement of difficult goals. Many bureaucratic organizations have solved the problem of discontent and dissension through clarification of superordinate objectives, adequate interface management, clarification of job descriptions, employee training and educational programs.

NASA (National Aeronautics and Space Administration) is an example of a bureaucratic organization that has been eminently successful in the achievement of national objectives, unfettered by the thwarting or distortion of communication and innovative ideas because of hierarchical divisions. Numerous other examples in both the government and the private sector can be brought to mind. The bureaucratic organization is designed to permit and encourage selection and promotion based on technical competence. But consider a Machiavellian manager whose personal ambitions for aggrandizement are allowed to override the organization's objectives, who disregards the designs and intention of the bureaucratic model, and, unmindful of the bureaucratic imperative calling for impartial interpersonal relations, promotes a subordinate who is interested only in his or her own personal welfare and who will ape the supervisor's philosophy and practices. Is the bureaucratic organization to be held responsible for this? Or is this not, in fact, an overt manifestation of the type of human behavior that we all encounter at times? It is this sort of behavior, this lack of values, this disregard for principles, that must be improved to make the bureaucratic organization the effective model it is designed to be. Imagine a group of similar individuals—carefully selected puppets—having the unsatisfactory characteristics just described, reaching a decision by consensus in a so-called democratic organization.

There is no denying that senior management in certain bureaucratic organizations is not utilizing to the full the human resources available because the subordinates have learned to mistrust senior management, because they have seen the exercise of reprisals, and have observed the success of coworkers whose opinions are swayed by the expectation of economic reward rather than by the defense of a principle.

As to the selection of incompetents, the old story of the personnel manager who hired as a secretary the young woman with outstanding physical attributes rather than the applicant who took dictation at 120 words a minute and transcribed the notes at the same rate, serves to point up the fact that is is one thing to know what should be done and quite another to do it. Arbitrary and zany rules are made by arbitrary and zany people. It happens that a predisposition to be arbitrary is a rather frequent characteristic of human behavior which exists in many organizations—a knowledge that can be utilized to advantage—and will, it appears, be as active twenty-five to fifty years from now as it is at present.

Confusion and conflict about rules and regulations can be clarified, if we so desire. Are the rules to apply equally to all, or is there to be some favoritism? Do we wish to communicate clearly to all our associates, or do we enjoy being so superior that no one understands us? Can we not even understand our own transcribed notes?

Unfair treatment of subordinates or associates is not confined to bureaucratic organizations. Try differing with top management in a university, for example. We need to improve human behavior if we are to achieve exemplary organizations, not seek other types of organizational models whose results will surely display the same detrimental forms of behavior. If a comedian like Charlie Chaplin can capture the absurdity of rigid hierarchical systems based on pseudologic and inappropriate rules, surely a trained manager can alter such a set of circumstances when he or she perceives them. It is hoped that, with enough experience, the manager may even learn not to allow such a set of circumstances to develop in the first place. This certainly should be an ideological goal for every system manager.

The question of the ability of bureaucratic organizations to assimilate the influx of new technology and scientists entering the organization can better be judged, if the reader recalls some of the rather remarkable feats accomplished by bureaucratic organizations, such as placing a man on the moon and other aerospace achievements, the continuing development of the artificial heart, nuclear power, and the electric automobile.

The individual today is in the enviable position of being very largely the master of his own destiny. He need not became what has been described as the dull, gray, conditioned organization man. Widespread educational opportunities have made it possible for each of us as individuals to be aware of the importance of personal objectives, of the necessity of plans to achieve these goals, and of the cost to us in time, effort, training, experience, and determination.

POSSIBLE ALTERNATIVES

In 1964, when a study was undertaken to project what conditions would be like in the United States after the year 1985, the research team found the problem of the analysis and prediction of national values highly difficult. A society as large as that in the United States, because of the complexity of its background, has a confused and often contradictory value orientation. The report, published by the Syracuse University Research Corporation, suggests that as the population becomes more homogeneous and more urbanized, more consistent value patterns may emerge, but, it admonishes, this is by no means certain. The report further states that in a fundamental sense, a plurality of values and value systems is the hallmark of political democracy, American variety. New additions to our value systems are continually being made. Note the recent addition to our society of some two hundred thousand "boat people"—by presidential decree.

In reporting the results of their research, the Syracuse team pointed out that the function of organizations and their management is the relating of human resources to economic goals. During the period from 1920 to 1964, theories of management were built around relatively simple and stable concepts of hierarchy in formal and informal organization, horizontal and vertical span or control, staff and line, work measurement, accountability, and efficiency. But, the research team found, the large-scale organizations of the 1960s and the larger and more complex organizations of the 1980s cannot be understood within the framework of these simplistic concepts. Therefore, the management of these vast and complex systems will be possible only within a theory of formal organization that allows for the following:

1. More decentralization with greater delegation of authority
2. Multiple hierarchies within the organization as contrasted with the present usual single pyramid of authority and accountability
3. Shared decision-making relationships, both within and among organizations, resulting in "tensions of mutuality"
4. Increased use of automatic control systems
5. More transnational organizations
6. More specialization, more professionalism, with the expectation of loyalty patterns to the professional rather than the work organization
7. More shared decisions by combinations of managers and specialists

More specifically, this projection pictures the manager of the future as having indefinite lines of responsibility and authority, with the result that the manager must bargain for what he or she gets, rather than direct it. Management will depend upon computers and other cybernetic machines, but, paradoxically, it will be far more concerned with human factors and personality feedbacks in the decision-making process.

The prototypes of this future organization are to be found in the Department of Defense in the 1960s and in the large-scale American university, or what has been called the "multiversity." These organizations are characterized both by size and a multiplicity of functions. The Syracuse report states that managers within these organizations are forced to adopt techniques and machines for enhancing overall control of the total system; but they are also forced to decentralize operations, deal with multiple hierarchies within the system, and relate to other systems in a tension of interdependency and competition. Negotiating, bargaining, and brokerage functions are essential managerial skills in such organizations. Goal setting becomes a complex and conditional exercise.

The report observes that although by 1985 management will have at its disposal far more sophisticated methods for the storage and retrieval of information, for intra- and inter-organizational communications, and for speedy transportation, these developments will make the life of the manager more complex. One of the paradoxes of the future is that while an increasing number of managerial decisions will be handled by automatic data processing, buttressed by clear and swift communication networks, the intelligent direction and coordination of large-scale systems will place an even greater premium than at present upon the wise, artful, and broadly experienced general manager in organizations characterized by operational decentralization. In short, the proposition that effective decentralization can occur only where organizational centralization has become efficient will have become increasingly recognized, not as a paradox but as a logical reality. (Author's note: This is, and has been, the situation in Department of Defense system management offices.)

As a consequence, by 1985 university and in-house development courses for executive talent at both the junior and mid-career level will be an accepted necessity. Such courses will stress new theories of organization, like those suggested above, and emphasize far more than at present the psychological and social aspects of management and communication.

Before addressing these prognostications, let us consider comments and alternatives projected by another researcher. Warren Bennis has stated (1966a) that bureaucracy thrives in a highly competitive, undifferentiated, and stable environment, and that it is a lack of adaptability to shifts in the environment which will lead to the demise of bureaucracy and to the collaspe of management as we now know it.

It is difficult to agree with Bennis's observation. The Department of Defense system program offices operate in a highly differentiated and unstable environment, as do their counterparts in the private sector. The system program offices of the Department of Defense—and let us not forget that the Department of Defense was cited as a prototype of the future organization by the Syracuse report—have repeatedly demonstrated their ability to adapt to environmental changes. Their system management offices are always looking into the future, extending technological barriers and frontiers, achieving system objectives in spite of decisions handed down from the Department of Defense—and higher—levels concerning performance, quantities, numbers, and other areas. The magnitude of the expenditures of the Department of Defense system program office and their impact on the American economy certainly justify whatever mandates are placed upon the system-management offices; nevertheless, the mandates require an exceptional quality of adaptability. In fact, the statement can be made without fear of contradiction that the most outstanding characteristic of a system management office *is* its adaptability to a swiftly changing environment. The experiences of system managers— gathered through questionnaires, interviews, and personal experience— repeatedly cite the difficulty of achieving decisions by *bargaining.* A decision that requires bargaining inevitably requires compromise. A system manger cannot achieve system objectives through compromise decisions.

Or, stated differently, the compromises must be made in the planning phase, so that the control phase constitutes a time-phasing of planned events.

Still another organizational model has been proposed—the "democratic" organization.

THE CONSENSUS ORGANIZATION

Warren Bennis, whom we have already mentioned and who is an outstanding behavioral scientist, with an enviable record of management experience, and significant contributor to the literature of organizational behavior, is perhaps the best-known champion of what is known as the democratic organization. He has best presented its case, and has done a great service by highlighting some of the deficiencies, already discussed, in the bureaucratic organization. Bennis has projected an image of the sort of democratic organization that he foresees developing in the future. He believes that "democracy is inevitable" (Bennis, 1966a).

The democratic organization, Bennis foresees, is an organization in which decisions are made by group consensus; that is, it will be the majority vote of the group that will implement decisions. Bennis sees the future organization as having unique characteristics: it will be temporary in nature with adaptive, rapidly changing groups organized to solve specific problems, the members of the group being composed of relative strangers, each diversely skilled professionally. The differentiation of individuals will therefore be by skill and by professional training, not according to rank. This is foreseen as an adaptive temporary group of diverse specialists linked together by coordination that will replace bureaucracy as we know it today. This temporary group will have a reduced commitment to the working or operative group, with an according reduction in group cohesiveness. Workers will be required to cope with rapid change, to live in temporary organizations, quickly establishing meaningful work relationships and then as quickly severing them. Bennis also foresaw that these conditions will be conducive to strains and tensions (Bennis, 1966b).

Bennis's projected organization of the future reminds one of the project organization, sometimes called a matrix organization, which is presently in use in many bureaucratic organizations today, more specifically in system or project management offices. The project or matrix organization, as we know it, exists for short periods of time—although admittedly these so termed temporary organizations frequently exist for many, many years; it is directed by a project manager, is composed of specialists—having allegiance not only to the project manager but to the permanent functional manager from whom the specialist was borrowed—and may or may not have been established to solve an immediate problem or to serve the project manager for an extended period of time. In 1966, Bennis forecast the wider use of the project form of organization—a collaboration of specialists. This projection has already come true. The project organization, however, has proved to be an effective part of the bureaucratic model of organization—not a replacement for it.

Two alternatives to the bureaucratic organization have already been described. The Syracuse report, mentioned earlier, states that large and complex organizations cannot be understood within the framework of some of the "relatively simple and stable concepts" of the traditional school of management. The behavioral school and the management science school have, however, added additional tools the system managers can apply to aid in understanding and controlling large and complex organizations. Because the system manager is particularly concerned with the management of complex systems, let us now examine the concept of system management.

System management is the management of technical, business, and human resources within a particular organization or system, including the planning and control of the conceptual phase, validation and definition phase, design and development phase, the production phase, and operational or customer-application phase, of a given hardware or software system. The planning must include the complementary functions of testing, logistic support, maintenance support, personnel training, operational training, and the activation of user or customer organizations. System management is, in other words, the planning and control of all components of a system to achieve system objectives. A system in this context may be defined as a relationship of environmental factors, human factors, financial and material factors, and such methodologies as cybernetics, computer application, communication theory, the social system conceptual scheme, comprised of environmental factors, organizational factors, behavioral factors, applied management philosophy, and the necessary leadership to pursue a desired organizational objective. System management then is the planning and control of the very many tangible and intangible components of a given system to achieve that system's objective. A system manager thus requires a high degree of technical skill, skill with human resources, and conceptual skill—the three basic skills of the effective administrator identified by Robert Katz.

The 1964 Syracuse report foresaw a theory of formal organization that calls for more decentralization with greater delegation. The recognition that the achievement of complex objectives by a very large number of people from different organizations is extremely difficult has brought about many expansions and additions and changes to management theory. System managers have already been made aware of the environmental factors impacting on the system that must be considered, in design and in application. Dealing with such a wide diversity of disciplines, organizations in widespread geographical areas, changing needs and demands from customers, including testing in widely separated geographical areas and use or application under many different environments, they have already experienced the necessity of more—even great—decentralization, with greater delegation of tasks and of authority. Since the 1964 Syracuse report visualized the Department of Defense as a prototype, it is safe to say that the organizational model of the future—system management—is already with us today, has existed for many years, and is now available for even more widespread application. Many companies in the aerospace industry, jet-engine industry, and other suppliers of the Department of Defense are already aware, and have utilized, the system management organization for many years now. Presumably because government agencies are perceived as bureaucratic, many industrial and commercial companies are reluctant to follow the lead of the Department of Defense system management organization. But in the words of football coach George Allen, "The future is now." Present management theory can certainly accommodate more decentralization and delegation of power.

To continue with a consideration of the projections in the Syracuse report, experience has shown that the system manager is able to deal successfully with multiple hierarchies within the overall system. In the Department of Defense the system manager has dealt with the "usual" pyramid of authority with the system manager at the apex, and additional advice or directives imposed by higher Department of Defense or national authority, and the other pyramids of authority found in the major contractors, and the additional pyramids found in the numerous subcontractors, the great number of pyramids found in the sub-subcontractors, and so forth. In addition, the system manager works through and with the rather formidable pyramids of authority found in the supporting—training, logistics, testing—and the user organizations. These pyramids have resulted in the recognition of many interfaces. The system manger even now must identify the many interfaces between pyramids of authority and in some cases specify contractually who is responsible for what at each major interface.

Shared decision-making relationships have existed for many years in the Department of Defense model of system management. These shared decisions, as far as objectives go, must be made in the planning—conceptual and developmental—phases. Attempts to make shared decisions in the control—acquisition and deployment—phases, which result in the system manager being forced to use many coordinative devices to compensate for his or her lack of authority, have proved unsuccessful. There is a dilution of technical objectives in instances where the system manager is forced to rely upon shared decision-making relationships. To repeat, shared decisions are best made in the conceptual and developmental planning phases; in the control phase, the system manager should not be forced to rely on shared decisions—compulsory staff advice certainly, but not shared decisions.

Robert H. Miles and W. Alan Randolph have observed that to have all organizational participants share in a decision is generally thought to be desirable and that the literature dealing with participative decision making and power equalization in organizations is *normatively-* and *value-oriented* (italics added). The assumption is that the greater the participation, the better for both the participants and the organization. But, they point out, that although it is possible that while more complete sharing of decision-making responsibility does lead to more legitimacy for both the decision and the decision-making system, the actual effect is that the greater the degree of participation, the more the real situation conforms to a centralized decision-making structure—in effect, an apparent paradox in centralization through majority rule. It may be added that Mauk Mulder and Henk Wilke demonstrated this effect in an experimental study.

The word "normative" is an interesting one, meaning relating to, confoming to, or prescribing norms. A normative forecast is one in which we begin with the *assumed* future conditions, or those conditions we wish to bring about, and then determine plans to achieve our normative objective—a predetermined, preknown aim or goal. The scientific method involves an observation or hypothesis, then gathering data or information concerning the hypothesis, analyzing the results and proving or disproving the hypothesis by experiments or tests. It is, of course, possible to "prove" a normative hypothesis that does not conform to reality or to the true condition or situation. Much very valuable research, however, has been accomplished through the pursuit of normatively established objectives. The very difficult task of the system manger is to determine what of theory he or she may apply and what of theory is or is not appropriate to a particular situation. The system manager must serve as a bridge to connect theory with practice.

The increased use of automatic control systems is a necessity. For some years, the Department of Defense system manager has had a control room that is an exact duplicate of the one at the prime contractor's plant, with all changes posted in one control room immediately transmitted to the other. Both rooms graphically display the status of each major subsystem and long lead-time items—and trouble spots. The interest is in what is not going as expected and what is being done about it—what is planned to bring the variance back into line. This is an example of a management automatic control system. Automatic control systems for machines and processes will also continue to be advanced and applied.

The increase in number of transnational organizations is already a reality. With increased trade with China and Russia, it appears the trend will continue.

With the increase in knowledge in many new areas of materials and technologies has come an increase in specialization. There has been a marked growth in professionalism, aided, no doubt, by the consumer movement to require the licensing of professionals in many areas and by attempts to determine the "ultimate" designer of a faulty product. Loyalty patterns exhibit a tendency to place loyalty to the professional organization above loyalty to the work organization. Recognition by one's peers, national or international, is an increasing objective of professionals, rather than recognition within the work organization.

The advance of technology in many, many areas has made necessary shared decisions by managers and specialists, usually in the planning phase but occasionally in the control phase—for example, the Three Mile Island incident of the commercial nuclear-reactor emergency. The system organization, and the shorter-lived project or matrix organization, have developed from the necessity of having specialized technical personnel to advise the project or system manager. Note the use of the phrase "to advise the project or system manager." More and more decisions are shared to the extent that the system manager relies on specialists for expert opinion. The development of the project management and system management philosophy of management has concurrently developed the need for system (or project) managers who are capable of conceptualizing the entire system and can lead in the integration of all the very diverse disciplines.

I myself am personally familiar with a large manufacturer of electrical and electronic products who not long ago boasted with pride, "We build the best components in the industry." A very short while later, he reorganized his entire operation shifting the emphasis from the component to the entire project or system. Such a change in emphasis from component to system results in managerial emphasis on the conceptual skill of the system manager. A successful system manager is able to conceptualize the entire operation. The manager of component development and manufacture has a parochial outlook, by comparsion.

UNFORTUNATE EXAMPLES OF BUREAUCRACY

The bureaucratic type of organization offers much to the administration of large systems. As we have already observed, however, the individuals who staff bureaucratic organizations show the same human characteristics as those who are nonmanagers. Some exhibit a high sense of moral values; others do not. Some possess a high degree of integrity; others do not. Ideally, only those who have a high sense of moral values and a high degree of integrity would be selected to become senior managers. Human judgment being fallible, however, some persons with little or no sense of moral values and little if any integrity ascend to senior positions. It is this small percentage of senior managers that gives the bureaucratic organization an unenviable reputation. The following examples are offered as illustrations of the effects of dysfunctional loyalties to groups rather than to the truth.

A patient with a history of symptoms of a specific infection went to the head of specialty clinic in a major military hospital. The clinic head had previously performed an operation on this patient. The operation was a controversial way of correcting a relatively common condition. The word "controversial" is used because many civilian physicians did not recommend the operation, using medication only to treat the symptoms. The patient described the symptoms, was examined internally, and told that there was "nothing wrong. It's all in your head." Three days later, due to incapacitating pain, the patient consulted a civilian specialist who, after examination, prescribed medication that not only alleviated the pain but cured the infection. A complaint to the head of the military hospital in question—a physician who, quite by chance, had trained in the specialty concerned—resulted in a four-hour interview with the patient, a review of the patient's medical history, which showed treatment by the original military physician for an infection which the hospital head said laboratory tests in the file did not confirm. The head of the hospital set up an appointment for the following day. On this occasion, he reviewed and criticized the medication prescribed by the civilian specialist. There was no attempt to find out why a staff specialist of the hospital had performed a controversial operation without consultation with other specialists, why the infection was erroneously treated, or why the subsequent infection was not diagnosed; in essense, why no effort was made to discover the facts. The head of the military hospital went to great lengths to defend the staff physician in spite of documentation proving the latter's incompetence. A search for the truth would have been far more producitve. After having agreed to consult the civilian specialist, the head of the military hospital failed to do so. Again, there was no search for the truth about the patient's past symptoms and condition. The consequences of a senior manager defending an incompetent in a situation where a medical facility serves thousands of people is obvious.

In the academic world, the bureaucratic organization also has had its share of managers who lack integrity and moral values. A new state university was founded to fill the educational needs of the people in a certain geographical area. State funds were provided to buy the necessary land, build the necessary buildings, hire the necessary faculty, and provide the necessary services. The board of trustees appointed a search committee to find the right candidates from which to choose a president for the university. The search committee screeened and interviewed a number of candidates, eliminated some whom they found unacceptable, and submitted to the board of trustees a list of names of those who were acceptable to the search committee and the faculty. Rumor has it that the list was returned to the search committee by the chairman of the board of trustees with instructions that the committee must include the name of one of the candidates that had already been eliminated. This candidate, having been added to the list, was then selected as president. How would you describe this "collegial" process? Some faculty members even decried the establishment of a search committee whose sole purpose proved only to do the bidding of the board of trustees. Again, it is the integrity of management (the individual managers performing under the policy of the senior managers) that determines the character—the image—of the organization, not the organizational model.

CHANCES OF ALTERATION IN HUMAN BEHAVIOR

The past practical experience of managers tends to contradict current theoretical ideas about future changes in human behavior. Some experts apparently expect that the behavior of human beings will change significantly in the next quarter or half century and thus enable consensus decisions to become a way of organizational life. Should such a remote possibility come to pass—that is, so significant a change in human behavior as to allow operative-level, knowledgeable consensus decisions—bureaucratic organizations will only be that much more effective.

According to Bennis (1966b), the democratic organization has the following characteristics:

1. complete two-way communication
2. reliance on consensus to manage conflict, rather than on compromise or coercion

3. individual prestige based on technical competence, not on power or influence

4. informal atmosphere with a warm and friendly climate and a team approach to organizational problems, through which conflicts are resolved on rational grounds

But is this model "democratic" organization too different from the objectives of the current bureaucratic organizations? The development and maintenance of two-way vertical or four-way vertical and horizontal communication have been one aim of bureaucratic organizations for a long time. There are many bureaucratic organizations where communication exists in all directions. Regardless of whether or not an organization is termed democratic, true communication will not exist unless conscious efforts are made to define and understand communication among hierarchical tiers. Some understanding obviously must now be developed as to those who have sufficient technical or managerial expertise to provide meaningful inputs into the communication channels. Unknowledgeable inputs can contribute nothing positive to the communication process. A voice that speaks merely to expound an opinion, a biased or an unfounded one, cannot essentially contribute to either the communication or decision processes.

Many people have contributed to the improvement of the communication process. Most of us are aware of the differences in *perception* that various people have, and may even recollect the much-told story of the four blind men who encountered an elephant and were asked to describe it. One, grasping the tail, said the beast felt like a rope. Another, encountering the side of the elephant, observed that it resembled a wall. Still another, feeling the legs, described the beast as being like a tree trunk. The one who had hold of the ear found that the elephant resembled a tent flap. Our interpretations are largely the result of background, knowledge, experience, and associations.

Sigmund Freud—the founder and outstanding exponent of psychoanalytical theory to explain human behavior—propounded that the human personality is composed of or determined by three forces: the id, ego, and superego. The id is the instinctual, both impulsive and basic. The superego shows the results of moral or societal resraints and tells the individual what the proper course of action is. The ego serves as a mediator between the impulses of the id and the moral restraints of the superego, striving to keep the person's actions within acceptable social bounds.

Eric Berne, who has simplified Freud's concepts with his own parallel explanations of the forces determining human personality and behavior, has matched the term *child* with Freud's id, *adult* with Freud's ego, and *parent* with Freud's superego. Berne, with the help of Thomas Harris, also developed a technique called transactional analysis, a technique of charting, either by conceptualizing or actually doing so on paper, the forces within a person from which a communication or interaction has emanated and the forces from within the second person by which the communication or interaction was perceived—or received. This technique quickly identifies the advantages of complementary transactions in which lines of communication or interaction are parallel as opposed to the disadvantages of crossed transactions, which result when one person "talks down" from his superior—or "parent"—force to the second person's inferior—or "child"—force. Although crossed transactions can also be caused by one person, the lower man on the totem pole, talking up to the other person, the use of the term "talking down" was selected to show in a simple and straightforward manner the necessity to consider the other person's perception of the message or interaction. Every manager of any organization can certainly improve his or her ability to communicate by considering the possible perceptions and the meanings of words imputed by those addressed, and thereby avoid the use of those words or voice intonations that are perceived as being "talked down to."

The purpose of the foregoing digression is to indicate that the manager of a bureaucratic organization can develop a communications system with whatever characteristics seem needed or desired.

Bennis foresaw reliance on consensus in organizational decision making in 1966. Continuing and commendable efforts since have been and are being made to bring the level of decision making down to the lowest organizational level in which necessary information and technical expertise exist. Attempts have also been made to allow many more to participate in the decision-making process. Participation is however, like the story of the four blind men and the elephant, differently perceived by different people. Participation does not necessarily mean rule by consensus. Meaningful participation exists when questions are raised, opinions voiced, advantages and disadvantages cited, and alternatives proposed. The effective system manager, guided by the principle of compulsory staff advice, will listen attentively to the voices of all qualified specialists, and make the decision based on his or her conceptualization of the entire system. A consensus decision made by individuals not possessing such a conceptualization of the entire system all too often fails to be effective. In this connection, it is interesting once again to note that in 1972, after Bennis had served as president of the University of Cincinnati, he modified his earlier opinion and observed that a viable managerial strategy does not rest in consensus.

Bennis's experience seems to parallel that of an earlier behavioral theorist,

Douglas McGregor. McGregor contributed theory X and theory Y to behavioral concepts. These two theories are actually two sets of assumptions—two extreme views—that management seems to have about workers. Theory X assumes that the labor force is lazy, must be closely supervised, and does not want responsibility; theory Y assumes that men and women work because they expect to, that they will accept responsibility and even seek it, and that all men and women possess creativity and are looking for a chance to express it. (McGregor later became a college president—president of Antioch College—and his service as chief executive was an eye-opening experience for him. He reported that from it he learned what no amount of observation of other people could have taught him [McGregor, 1954]). System managers who have been forced to rely on such coordinative devices as committees or boards for decisions have come to the same conclusion. The point being emphasized here is that maximum participation should and must be encouraged so that the accountable system manager, after having carefully considered the opinions of all qualified technical advisors—even though the opinions may be in direct opposition to each other—can then make those decisions that are most effective from an overall point of view.

The idea that power and influence should be based on technical competence and knowledge is not entirely recent. Many engineering-oriented organizations have two ladders of advancement—the technical and the managerial. The technical ladder leads to increased pay, status, and influence. Sometimes a technical employee will be better paid than the manager who is his superior. Thus, it may sometimes be one of a manager's less desirable tasks to overrule some engineering or scientific genius when the former knows of economic, social, political, or other reasons that necessitate overriding a purely technically directed position. For this and other reasons, a manager or his staff must accumulate knowledge in every area bearing on a decision. The technical manager of today needs more than just technical expertise—human skills and conceptual skills are equally important.

Some behavioral scientists have recommended an organizational atmosphere that permits and encourages emotional expression (Bennis, 1966b). If by emotional expression is meant the right to speak one's dissenting opinion on decisions in a loud continuous manner, the resultant atmosphere might well prove highly detrimental to the achievement of the organization's objectives, particularly in a large system. Any manager must have self-control and self-discipline before he or she can perform an adequate job in directing the efforts of others. Is it too much to ask that all employees practice similar self-control? The process of selecting both staff and workers looms as ever more and more important for success in system management.

Conflict does not merely occur between management and employees but between various individuals in the organization, both vertically and horizontally. Any bureaucratic organization, by definition, tries to select and promote on the basis of technical competence and seeks to prevent interpersonal relationships from entering into the decision-making process. As long as human kind remains as it is, however, there must be a series of checks and balances in every organization. Conflict occurs even in the academic world when a given individual, perhaps a faculty member, has a grievance, maybe even a purely personal one, and finds no formally constituted grievance procedure on which to fall back. Surely the growth of the American Association of University Professors and the American Federation of Teachers is not a matter of happenstance. In this regard, the bureaucratic organization, with its hierarchies, is better designed to protect the rights of the individual—whether he or she is in a management position, and thus perceived as part of the establishment, or is a supervised employee who relies on some exterior bureaucratic organization, such as a union, to help protect his or her rights.

The authority relationship in the bureaucratic organization follows the familiar pyramidal structure. Some observers believe that the numerous organizations a system manager must deal with lie outside this pyramid—due to the fact, for example, that Department of Defense system managers must deal with civilian contractors, other military commands, civilian subcontractors, and frequently other government agencies. These relationships, however, do include the usual pyramidal structure in each of the usually autonomous agencies supporting the system manager, but the concept of system management requires the imposition of a superordinate authority system, encompassing all participating organizations, with the system manager at the apex. Of course, this concept has not been without its problems. The discussion in later chapters will document some of the problems and some of the less than successful ways used to overcome them. The superordinate authority relationship has become well established, with the authority relationship and other concepts spelled out by means of contractual documents covering important interfaces between organizations that usually have no common authority relationship.

Bennis has very accurately foreseen the modification of organizations to improve communication, to recognize the technical competence of individuals, to develop a warm, friendly, informal organizational atmosphere and a team approach to organizational problems. The system approach relies on authority rather than consensus to manage conflict, chiefly because only the system manager and members of his or her immediate staff have the conceptual vision to make an effective decision for the overall system. The lack of such superordinate authority has in the past resulted in compromise decisions, but steps have been taken to correct this deficiency. Later research and theory have tended to justify the earlier actions of system managers.

For yet another unhappy example of the type of behavior that many people seem to expect of a bureaucratic organization, consider a committee of four members who are to determine the best way to accomplish a task. Imagine—not unrealistically—that one member possesses neither the knowledge nor background to contribute to the decision, that a second member is soon leaving the organization and really does not care, or worse, would like to see the organization saddled with a poor decision, that a third member has vested interests at stake, and that the fourth is purely and simply an observer for senior management. This last member possesses no understanding of the subject area for the decision, but his interest is in reporting back to his benefactors the positions and arguments of the other members of the committee. This description of an imaginary committee, largely comprised of puppets, points up the fact that committee decisions—consensus decisions—are not necessarily democratic. The assignment of mediocre participants to a committee—or the assignment of those whose views can be controlled or are already fixed—to make recommendations concerning a course of action or inaction desired by senior management is not an example of democratic process. A committee composed of mediocre individuals, rather than of individuals well qualified by knowledge and experience, will certainly not be brash enough to express opinions that differ from those who control the organization and established the committee, if experience has shown that senior management expects a certain decision—not necessarily the best working one. Perhaps senior management is looking to a committee to "legitimatize" earlier actions or decisions of senior management. Consensus decisions in the *controlled* (democratic?) organization are prone to reflect senior management philosophy, sense of values, desires, and expectations—to be an extension of the status quo rather than a sincere attempt, through examination of conflicting alternatives, to reach the best solution or possibly an intelligent compromise. The long-term interests and objectives of the organization deserve to be served rather than the fear of holding an opinion that differs from senior management's. In a truly free environment the most qualified participants, from the standpoint of knowledge and experience, would be appointed to a decision-making committee, and the decision would be arrived at by a truly democratic process. The committee decision would then be implemented by senior management.

The foregoing discussion emphasizes, once again, the fact that the organization, whether bureaucratic or otherwise, is a reflection of the character, integrity, dedication, and devotion of the senior management, or, conversely, the lack of these attributes. Changing the form of an organization will not change the character, philosophy, policies, and practices of its managers. Human nature being as it is, and unlikely to change drastically in the near future and but slowly in the foreseeable one, the bureaucratic type of organization seems presently the structure best suited to provide fair and just treatment for all concerned.

Desirable or not, manipulative, unscrupulous managers who practice "Do unto others before they do unto you" exist and will continue to exist as long as the end results of their efforts support the real objectives of those who control the organization. The bureaucratic organization, managed by people of integrity and dedicated to the achievement of the organization's objectives, making use of internal or external audit agencies to insure an adequate adjudicative process, offers to both management and employees an environment of integrity and security. It is those not adequately qualified by knowledge, experience, and moral character who give the bureaucratic organization an undesirable reputation—not the form of the organization.

ADVANTAGES OF BUREAUCRATIC ORGANIZATION

Peter Blau, another social scientist, has found that bureaucracies are less rigid structures than popularly supposed. Bureaucratic organizations do not remain fixed according to a formal blueprint, but are always evolving into new forms. Conditions change; problems arise; and in the course of coping with them, the members of the organization establish new procedures and often tranform their interrelationships, thereby modifying the structure.

Thus a bureaucracy can be defined as an institutionalized method of organizing social conduct in the interest of administrative efficiency (Blau). The chief problem is how to remove expeditiously recurrent obstacles to efficient operations. This cannot be accomplished by a system of rigid preconceived procedures but only by creating conditions favorable to continuous adjustive development in the organization. But to establish such a pattern of self-adjustment in a bureaucracy, conditions must prevail that encourage its members to cope with emergent problems and find solutions on their own initiative that will obviate the need for unofficial practices which thwart the objectives of the organization (Blau).

Blau has identified five conditions that are necessary for adjustive development:

1. job security
2. standards of performance
3. cohesive work groups
4. evaluation on the basis of achieving given objectives
5. separation of the management of operations from the determination of employment conditions.

Elaborating on this last point, Blau explains that many employees fear that high work performance and productivity will result in their losing their jobs. An example of the wisdom of the separation of management of operations from the determination of employment conditions can be seen in the customary practice of government agencies where such procedures as the selection, promotion, discharge, and salary of employees are determined by civil-service commissions and are in no way involved with day-to-day operations. Thus, the conditions of employment are neither set nor enforced by the immediate supervisor.

The managers of government bureaucratic organizations have many advantages over managers of private-sector bureaucratic organizations. In government agencies, job security is not a matter of paramount concern to the employee. In the private sector, blue-collar workers have gained job security through union contracts and grievance procedures, but although some professional employees have the security offered by union contracts, many professional and most white-collar employees do not.

Standards of performance, particularly when negotiated between supervisor and employee, are in widespread use nowadays. The bureaucratic organization, whether governmental or private, is in a position to develop and apply standards of performance if management so desires.

The bureaucratic model of organization has had a long and successful history of operation. During World War II, our government was faced with the need to establish a crash program for the development of the atomic bomb. The success of the Manhattan Project operation—a forerunner of the system management organization—which was created under Major General Leslie R. Groves, is a vivid demonstration of the effectiveness of the bureaucratic form of organization to adapt to radical technological change and the rapid assimilation of scientific personnel. In fact, Leslie Groves has reported that the five major factors which made the Manhattan Project a successful operation were (1) a specific objective; (2) a breakdown of the organization into task assignments with those responsible individuals identified; (3) delegation of authority with responsibility; (4) utilization of agencies already in existence—no empire building; (5) the project, backed by the full authority of the federal government, had access to a nearly infinite potential in scientists, engineers, and production specialists and what appeared to be an almost unlimited supply of people of ingenuity and determination. The development of these factors, credited by General Groves as keys to the successful development of the atomic bomb on an accelerated basis during World War II, is good advice for any system manager today.

A review of the crash program by NASA in successfully fulfilling the national objective of the 1960s in putting men on the moon and returning them successfully—the latter more than doubling the original feat in complexity—is another example of the adaptability and effectiveness of the bureaucratic form of organization.

BUREAUCRATIC ORGANIZATION AND THE FUTURE

Richard Shomper and Victor Phillips, Jr., have studied the problems of the bureaucratic organization, its managers, and its operative employees. Their assumption and conclusion are that bureaucracy will continue for the time being as the usual organizational framework in Western society. Some of their suggestions to those managers who occupy top-level positions in bureaucratic organizations are as follows:

1. provide incentives to improve morale and productivity
2. incorporate contemporary management theory at all levels of the organization
3. develop tests to select managers skilled in human relations
4. develop criteria for evaluating managerial skills that should be coordinated with the evaluator and the evaluated at the beginning of the rating period—the evaluation should include the manager's effect upon his or her subordinates
5. reward outstanding performance
6. decentralize
7. eliminate negative incentives
8. design and implement an effective management development program

Both practical experience and social research have shown that the bureaucratic organization is, and will continue to be, a viable framework for the management of large and complex systems attempting to achieve difficult objectives. Unquestionably system managers will continue to work with the bureaucratic form of organization for a long time to come. Thus, it behooves any system manager to become familiar with the advantages and disadvantages of the model, to implement the recommendations for improvement, and to work toward making the bureaucratic organization an even more effective administrative tool.

Changes—really significant changes—in management behavior came slowly. A news item reinforcing this observation is summarized herewith. At the 1975 symposium entitled "Man and Work in Society," jointly sponsored by the Western Electric Corporation and Harvard University, more than one hundred behavioral scientists had a field day, speculating on the effects on today's workplace and the workplace of the future of the pioneering Hawthorne studies. The reader may recall that the Hawthorne studies indicated that there were psychological factors that were of greater importance to productivity than exterior working conditions. These psychological factors included informal groups, informal relationships, social patterns, communication patterns, and the existence of informal leadership. The studies found that workers in groups set their own production and behavioral norms. The ninety industry representatives in attendance at the fiftieth anniversary of the beginning of the Hawthorne studies were extremely wary of suggesting that any changes in overall management style and in job structure had resulted from the findings of the Hawthorne studies or were in prospect for the future on a wide basis. Only a relative handful of the nation's working population is currently involved in experiments dealing with job enrichment or participative decision making. Money is still regarded as the primary work motivator. One lapse of authoritarianism that does appear to be making headway is the growing use of "flexitime" in which, within set limits, employees can pick their own arrival and departure times (*Production* magazine, 1975).

3 ... ORGANIZATIONAL CONFLICT
A Vertical Perspective

INTRODUCTION

Conflict as a subject of research and discussion in system management is relatively new. This chapter examines some of the results of that research and the implications of these results for the system manager.

There are some social scientists who believe that conflict—at least, some forms of conflict—may be beneficial. Morton Deutsch, for example, has stated that conflict is not inherently destructive, that since conflict is present in nearly all organizations, it must have many postive functions, that it prevents stagnation, stimulates interest, is a medium through which problems can be aired and solutions arrived at, and lies at the heart of personal and social change. Let us review the observations.

Each person's perception of conflict must of necessity influence his or her reaction to it; but the word "conflict" does not refer to differences in professional opinion which are freely expressed to help develop the policy or plans of an organization. One definition of conflict, in the sense that it is used here, is that behavior which is expended in opposition to other members (James Thompson). Another definition is that conflict exists whenever incompatible activities occur (Deutsch).

When human beings interact, there is usually the probability of latent or open conflict—at least to some degree. Indeed, the amount of organizational conflict is so high that a large amount of research into its nature, case, and results has been and continues to be done. As Claggett Smith pointed out, once intergroup conflict was recognized as a characteristic phenomenon and not simply a manifestation of irrationality preventing the cooperative functioning of bureaucratic organizations, increasing attention has been devoted to its management. Smith's own research complemented other studies of intraorganizational conflict and its consequences. His basic premise is that the source of intraorganizational conflict lies in the very nature of the organization as a social system, the way the system is structured, and how its component subsystems are interrelated. He further states that the effects of structural variables in generating interlevel conflict are mediated by interpersonal processes, and that the effect of intraorganizational conflict on organizational functioning partly depends upon the mechanisms used to manage or control it.

Perhaps conflict is not inherently pathological or destructive, but its results for the system manager are dysfunctional. Does the fact that conflict is so pervasive mean that it has positive functions? Or, in sum total, do the disadvantages of conflict outweigh the advantages, if any, for the system manager? Conflict may prevent stagnation, but are there not more positive ways for the system manager to prevent stagnation? Perhaps conflict stimulates interest and curiosity, but must conflict be the medium by which problems are aired and solutions arrived at? Cannot matters be brought to the attention of those concerned without waiting for conflict to arise? Again, conflict may be the root of needed social change, but this fact does not make conflict desirable to the system manager. Social change has resulted from conflict in past history. We have seen recent social changes initiated as a result of conflict. Does this mean that conflict is the only or most desirable agent for change?

Morton Deutsch has stated that conflict is often part of the process of testing and assessing oneself and, as such, may be highly enjoyable as one experiences the pleasure of the full and active use of one's capacities. This, and the fact that some men and women find the process highly enjoyable, are conceded. But the question remains, Does this testing process have a place in system management? For participants in system management, the full and active use of one's capacities may better be found in the enthusiastic support of the group's and the organization's objectives.

Conflict demarcates groups from one another and thus helps to establish group and personal identity; external conflict often fosters internal cohesiveness (Deutsch). But system managers will do well to demarcate groups, one from the other, by means other than conflict—and fuctional groupings serve well. Of course, conflict caused by external forces may foster internal cohesiveness, but so will superordinate organizational or system objectives.

The reader is again invited to consider the observations of Miles and Randolph that the literature dealing with decision making and power equalization is normatively and value oriented. It appears that much of the literature concerning some conflict is also normatively and value oriented.

SOME CONFLICT TO BE EXPECTED

Intergroup conflict in organizations has been attributed to problems of communication between those involved, to differences in basic interests and goals, and to a lack of shared perceptions and attitudes among members at different echelons (Smith). A number of researchers have found that achieving adequate interlevel communication is an inherent problem in any large complex organization. Organizational size inevitably gives rise to specialization and a proliferation of organizational tasks. Because of this, increasing reliance is placed upon supervisory roles, and the supporting staff functions to achieve the necessary coordination. But achieving coordination in this way often has the effect of placing further impediments on the flow of information. On the positive side, however, studies to increase management's ability to communicate have resulted in many improvements—training in the technique of transactional analysis, to name but one.

Conflict has been viewed by some as stemming essentially from basic differences of interests between participants occupying different positions in the organizational hierarchy (Smith). Another view emphasizes that conflict arises not simply from misunderstandings, but from differences among subgroups who are in functional competition with each other, rationally pursuing different goals and struggling for limited organizational rewards (Daniel Katz). Such differences are inherent in a hierarchical organization (Smith). The increase in supervisory or leadership roles, together with the accompanying delegation of authority, leads to increased centralized control. As a consequence of the disproportionate representation of the interests of the leaders, such centralized control has the effect of displacing organizational goals, so that they are reflected even less in the attitudes of those lower in the hierarchy.

Hierarchical organization increases the disparity between those in authority and those with technical competence and their share in the rewards of the organization (Victor Thompson). As a result, most participants become less committed to the organization and fail to accept its goals. Yet the reader can surely visualize the multiplicity of problems that arise when all participants of the system are not accountable to the system manager or instances where the system manager does not hold the allegiance of all participants. Successful system managers use superordinate goals, with clearly defined individual goals for each subordinate unit or functional group to achieve system objectives. Cooperation with other specified units is listed as an objective for each unit or group.

In discussing intergroup conflict, which is attributed to a lack of shared perceptions and attitudes among members of different echelons, some researchers view member consensus as arising primarily through processes of cohesiveness and participation in the larger group or organization (Smith). Participation, particularly when communication channels are adequate, permits members to ascertain the norms of the organization and other echelons. Under conditions of high cohesiveness, members will be motivated to accept influence attempts and to adhere to normative prescriptions. A variant of this view would also highlight the importance of shared perceptions and attitudes in the prevention of conflict, but would stress the importance of preprogramming of consensus through very careful selection of personnel for organizational roles.

The tendency for conflict to escalate is caused by the conjunction of three interrelated processes: (1) competitive processes involved in the attempt to win the struggle; (2) processes of faulty and biased perception; and (3) commitment to a given course of action arising out of pressures for cognitive and social consistency (Deutsch).

The system manager should encourage competition but only on the impersonal professional level. Communications about the organizational goals of each "competing" group should always contain specific references to cooperation with other specific groups in order to attain overall system goals. The system manager should include in performance evaluations of subordinate managers a consideration of the degree of cooperation achieved in working with other lateral managers and groups. Faulty and biased perceptions can be remedied by the frequent communication of overall goals and the recognition and statement of the activities of each group involved in the entire system management process. The system manager should recognize the professional achievements of individuals and functional groups in such a way as to stress the contribution these have made to the success of the system. Such techniques have proved successful in developing a commitment to system objectives.

There are other factors that may serve to limit and encapsulate conflict, so that a spiraling intensification does not develop. Such factors are the number and strength of the existing cooperative bonds, crosscutting identifications, common allegiances and memberships among the conflicting parties; the existence of values, institutions, procedures, and groups that are organized to help limit and regulate conflict; and the salience and significance of the costs of intensifying conflict (Deutsch). Again, superordinate goals, recognition of and stress on individual and group performances that contribute to the success of system objectives, and the recognition of cooperative action serve to eliminate, reduce, or restrict activity that might otherwise result in harmful conflict. The system manager must prevent the development of win-or-lose conflict situations.

The purpose of the present discussion is to provide the system manager with an insight into the causes of conflict and where it may be expected to occur, in order to plan for and circumvent it. That may well prove more difficult than it seems. Lyman Bryson has observed that in a bureaucracy ideas do not stand or fall on their merits alone, that it is not only the idea or opinion that wins but also the man or woman behind it. Bryson found this condition to be inherently competitive rather than cooperative. Kurt Lewin has pointed out that competition attacks group solidarity and consequently the ability of the group to employ specialization in pursuit of the group goal. Victor A. Thompson's research found that in a formally structured group, the idea man or woman is doubly dangerous: first, such a person endangers the established distribution of power and status; second, he or she is perceived as a competitive threat to his or her peers. As a result, those with ideas tend to be suppressed. Thompson finds that, as a result of the antipathy to idea independence and to brilliance which he found pervasive in bureaucracies, the average person who will get along with others and go along with the system is preferred. Here again, the job of the system manager is a challenging one. He must seek idea men to achieve the system objectives but at the same time guard against the antipathy toward brilliance.

DIMENSIONS OF CONFLICT

It appears conceptually advantageous to consider system conflict as being of at least two types, vertical and horizontal. In either vertical or horizontal dimensions, system conflict may be both intraorganizational and interorganizational. Hierarchical organization increases the disparity between authority, technical competence, and a share in the rewards of the organization (Victor Thompson). In the usual system there may be a number of organizations in the hierarchy because of the tiers of system director, prime or major contractor or contractors, turn-key contractors, subcontractors, sub-subcontractors, etc. Possibly, proper contractual terminology can reduce vertical conflict between otherwise unrelated organizations. Under any arrangement, the management of the interfaces generated between organizations becomes increasingly important.

The horizontal dimension of system conflict is challenging. The system manager usually has coordinative tasks to accomplish with lateral managers in various functional agencies over which the manager has no authority relationship. The project manager concept has served to highlight this difficulty.

For purposes of conceptualization, investigation, and discussion, types of conflict among the subunits of formal organizations have been identified. Three additional types of subunit conflict identified by Louis R. Pondy are (1) bargaining conflict among the parties to an interest-group relationship or the bargaining model, (2) bureaucratic conflict between the parties to a superior-subordinate relationship or the bureaucratic model (vertical), and (3) stress conflict among parties to a lateral or working relationship or to the system model (horizontal).

Pondy's report continues that bargaining conflict is a result of a discrepancy between aggregated demands of the competing parties and the available resources. The bargaining model or interest-group model is concerned with conflict arising from competition. A major element in strategic bargaining is that of attitudinal structuring whereby each party attempts to secure the moral backing of relevant third parties, for example, the public or the government. The bargaining model is visible throughout the system management process. Even though the system manager has directive power, it is frequently desirable to resort to the bargaining model to allow all participants maximum inputs. If the bargaining process should fail, the system manager must resort to his directive powers.

CAN CONFLICT BE CONSTRUCTIVE?

There are differing views of the desirability of conflict in organizations. A number of types of organizations have been identified. Three general types and their characteristics are as follows (Victor Thompson): (1) An ideological organization to perpetuate certain beliefs, e.g., the Women's Christian Temperance Union; (2) the giant enterprise with nonideological purposes employing highly subdivided technologies, not confining its activities to a local community; and (3) the local enterprise employing highly elaborated, differentiated technologies, differing from the giant enterprise in markets or clientele. Markets tend to be restricted to the same geographical territory that supplies the labor force and other resources. The system manager is less often concerned with an ideological or local enterprise.

In the development of this book an a priori assumption has been made that both vertical and horizontal conflict should be reduced, because my own past experience has demonstrated that conflict in system management is not constructive and is to be avoided. Various causes of conflict, both internal and external, have been identified in order to assist the system manager. An unusually large number of findings have been reported to justify the contention that conflict is usually dysfunctional and to be avoided. At least, the reader will have been exposed to the research and findings of a large number of competent individuals.

Constructive conflict may exist in certain types of giant enterprises. For instance, one researcher finds that in the automobile distribution system, i.e., factory-dealer relationship, there are five conditions conducive to constructive conflict (Assael):

1. Organizations should encourage a continuous reappraisal of policies.

2. Organizations within the system must be willing to communicate objectives and insure constant feedback. Insufficient communication can produce misunderstanding and a denial of the legitimacy of organizational objectives.

3. Member organizations must be willing to redefine allocation of resources and division of labor in light of long-term organizational goals.

4. The disputants should promote systematic resolution of conflicts, relying on self-regulatory procedures rather than on appeals to government. Great advances have been made in attempts to manage conflict by exchange of views, most notably through dealer-relation committees and policy readjustments.

5. Interaction that encourages self-restraint in the use of power by the dominant organization facilitates conflict resolution. The arbitrary use of power would seem to preclude constructive results, since the subordinated elements may eventually reject the legitimacy of management directives.

Should these conditions not prevail, there is the danger that a substantial segment of the dealer population may no longer feel economically motivated to remain in the system. High dealer turnover and lack of representation in certain areas would mean a weakening of the manufacturer's basic link to the consumer. Such destructive consequences must be avoided by insuring constructive channels for conflict (Assael).

Claggett Smith states that although in some instances conflict can be so intense that it destroys an organization, in other instances it can stimulate creative problem solving and innovation. Another finding suggests that when the conflicts consist of differences in ideas and approaches, in contrast to differences in values and basic motivations, then it may have a constructive and stimulating effect (Evan).

Are differences in ideas and approaches a conflict? In a professional organization they should not be. Eugene Litwak reports that the traditional bureaucratic organization can tolerate very little conflict; the human relations organization somewhat more; the professional organization, a great deal; and he notes that the potential for conflict tends to be greater in the centralized bureaucratic organization. It would seem, however, that the conflict he instances is more in the nature of differences in professional opinion, not behavior by organization members expended in opposition to other members.

Morton Deutsch finds that there are a number of reasons why a co-operative process is likely to lead to productive conflict resolution: (1) it aids open and honest communication of relevant information between the participants; (2) it encourages the recognition of the legitimacy of each other's interests and of the necessity of searching for a solution that is responsive to the needs of each side; (3) it leads to a trusting, friendly attitude that increases sensitivity to similarities and common interests, while minimizing the salience of differences.

The reader has now been exposed to my a priori assumption that conflict in system management is to be avoided and to research results which indicate that under certain conditions, in certain types of organizations, at certain times, conflict may be constructive. Let us consider vertical conflict in more detail.

VERTICAL CONFLICT

Conflict in the vertical dimension or conflict among those in a superior-subordinate authority relationship is often referred to as bureaucratic conflict; it usually arises because superiors attempt to control the behavior of subordinates, and subordinates resist such control (Pondy). The bureaucratic, hieratic, or authority-structured form of organization is particularly concerned with vertical conflict problems. Mayer N. Zald has also found that conflict is most likely to occur between units that are unable to control their situation and those who are perceived as being in control. According to Chester Barnard's acceptance theory of authority, a successful authority relationship is marked by the set of activities over which the subordinate has willingly surrendered to a superior the right to exercise discretion. Of course, the system manager must remember that he or she has to earn the respect of the subordinate organizations, groups, and individuals in system management. And he or she should likewise be aware of the existence of Barnard's acceptance theory in order better to understand the behavior of subordinates.

System managers delegate authority to subordinates in order to enable the subordinate manager to complete assigned tasks to the best of the subordinate's ability. As the subordinate assumes responsibility—the obligation to perform the tasks enumerated to the best of his or her ability—so is he or she held accountable (the requirement to report progress being made toward assigned and willingly assumed goals).

The consequences of intraorganizational conflict in the functioning of an organization depends to a large extent upon the processes employed to control or manage the conflict (Smith). The strategies utilized for dealing with various types of conflict range from those that simply attempt to make the system work to those that involve restructuring the organization in order to reduce built-in conflict (Daniel Katz). According to Claggett Smith, in a highly structured organization where there is a need for joint decision making, the possibility of conflict increases.

Victor Thompson in his research on hierarchy, specialization, and organizational conflict found that technological specialization when combined with the bureaucratic model of organization produces a pattern of conflict, caused by the gap between authority and the perception of technical needs and the fact that these two elements are in the hands of two separate sets of officials. According to Thompson, intraorganizational conflict results from (1) disagreement over the necessity of authoritatively created interdependence, (2) growing disparity between rights and abilities, (3) seemingly unreasonable dependencies, and (4) differences in value and reality perceptions. A look at the process of system management shows that the necessity for the system manager to have sufficient authority to enable the direction of diverse activities—and organizations— to achieve the final objective is recognized to the extent that contractual documents spelling out authority and accountability relationships are currently in use. The project organization or problem-solving approach reduces the disparity between rights and abilities. The superordinate system objective points out the fact that each organization must success-fully complete its assigned goals. Improved communication channels and techniques enable the system manager to instill a set of values that will help to weld the personnel working toward given system objectives into a cohesive group with an open appreciation of each individual and each group's contribution.

According to Thompson, two important elements affecting human behavior in the bureaucratic organization are the social process of speciali-zation and the cultural institution of hierarchy. He finds that the good things—the satisfactions or rewards—the organization may have to offer are distributed according to hierarchical rank or status. These good things include money, power, deference, interesting activities and associations, inside knowledge, convenience, and the like. Because these rewards are distributed according to status, and access to advancement in rank is controlled by hierarchical position, positions of authority acquire great power, become great personal prizes, and are therefore the objects of constant struggle.

In the years that have elapsed between Thompson's research and the present, some interesting changes in the bureaucratic organization have occurred: (1) the process of selection of managers and other personnel has improved; (2) the "dual ladder" of progression has been initiated and found successful in a number of technically oriented bureaucratic organizations. Under the dual-ladder progression, a person who is subordinate to a supervisor or manager may well be receiving economic rewards, status, and recognition far surpassing that accorded to the manager.[1]

In our modern Western democratic culture most organizational conflict arises because of the demands of subordinates for personal dignity, to be treated on the basis of merit, and to enjoy extra organizational freedom from organizational superiors—all rights that are ambiguous because they conflict with superordinate rights. This conflict has yet to be worked out in our culture (V. A. Thompson); the doctrines of democracy and liberalism that underlie much of our society have made almost no impact upon our bureaucratic organizations.

The very term "democracy" deserves some expansion here. The so-called democratic organization, as we have seen, is a term originally coined by Warren Bennis to describe the sort of future organization he envisioned, one characterized by consensus decisions at the lowest hierarchical level. Others, using the adjective "democratic" in the usual sense, see no reason why bureaucratic organizations can not be democratic in the sense that opinions are freely asked and given, but without the expectation of consensus decisions. As we have already indicated, it is difficult to see how system management organizations can ever be effectively conducted on the basis of consensus decisions: this does not mean that the opinions of all participants in an advisory sense should not be solicited. Managers of system organizations understand the necessity for reaching objectives through authority structures, hierarchy, and accountability, and accept these responsibilities when accepting the management position. Similarly, the employee should surely be made aware of his or her expected contribution, his or her responsibilities, the organizational objectives for the individual and the individual's group, and the expected contributions of the individual to the group and larger organization. Everyone has the option of accepting or declining an offer to perform a given piece of work. Once a position has been accepted, there is a moral obligation to satisfactorily perform.

Another variable affecting human behavior in organizations is the implications that one individual imputes to another. People impute superior abilities to persons of higher status (Barnard, 1946). Furthermore, this

---

1.   Victor A. Thompson suggests that for a discussion of the various psychological "goods" or advantages enjoyed by the person with the superior power in a relationship, see John W. Thibant and Harold H. Kelley, *The Social Psychology of Groups* (Wiley, New York, 1959), pp. 116-119.

imputed superior ability is then generated into a halo of general superiority. Thus, persons who have a very high status are called upon to solve problems of every conceivable kind, problems about which they may have no knowledge whatsoever. In political affairs this halo of high status causes people to speak out on all sorts of matters from a position of almost complete ignorance. The system manager must be on guard to prevent slipping into the position of expert on subjects in which he or she has no competence. Similarly, the system manager must both seek and accept advice from qualified experts. Conflict with expert functional groups quickly develops when the latter are given directives or decisions reflecting ignorance or misinformation. No system manager should ever be found in the same position as that of the academic vice-president of a university whose lack of ability, knowledge, and integrity was so widely recognized that the next hierarchical level—the academic deans—met behind his back and without his knowledge in an attempt to make consensus decisions. The thought was, of course, to present the vice-president with a plan or a decision—on the surface unanimous—so that he would accept the decisions without challenge or changes.

According to Victor Thompson, there are four principal behavioral systems whose interactions contribute to intraorganizational vertical conflict. These are the system of rights or authority, the system of deference or status, the system of specialization, and the system of communicative interaction. He identifies the bases of intraorganizational conflict as follows:

1. Conflict is a function of disagreement over the reality of interdependence, which is itself a result of differing perceptions of reality. Differing perceptions are a result of position in the authority and status system and in the system of person-to-person communication.

2. Conflict is a function of the degree of disparity between authority and the ability to contribute to goals. This arises from dependence upon specialists and the process of specialization.

3. Conflict is a function of the degree of status violation in interaction. Status violation results from growing interdependence of high and low status positions and dependence upon specialists.

4. The intensity of conflict depends on how much the manager's dependence upon the specialist affects the success of the organization.

5. Conflict results from a lack of shared values and reality perceptions, a lack of spontaneity and freedom in communicative interaction—which in itself is a result of the resistance to penetration from outside the organization of the principal behavioral systems: authority, status, and specialization.

6. Conflict results from extraorganizational influences that shape personality, group affiliations, racial and religious attitudes, and the like.

The system manager should realize then that conflict arises from growing inconsistencies between technical specialists and managerial roles.

Victor Thompson also found that in modern organizations the resolution of conflict was made difficult by the fact that it must either occur informally, by surreptitious and somewhat illegal means, or be repressed, creating a phony atmosphere of good feeling and superficial harmony. Such procedures are unthinkable for the present-day system manager.

Today a successful system manager must be aware of the conditions that are conducive to conflict and plan measures to reduce its likelihood; recognizing that such a situation is developing, he or she must take steps to prevent a confrontation with all its win-or-lose implications and resulting psychological scars. Should a confrontation occur, the system manager must make clear to the individuals or groups concerned that the objectives of the system are paramount and that the performance ratings of the individuals or group supervisors will reflect their attempts at cooperation. The managerial grid of Blake and Mouton (discussed in Chapter 4) and the transactional-analysis techniques of Harris can help to prepare the system manager to prevent conflict situations through analysis and proposed solutions.

Louis Pondy has identified three basic types of latent conflict: (1) competition for scarce resources, (2) drives for autonomy, and (3) divergence in subunit goals. These basic types are very important to the system manager because in the system management process itself there is generally competition for scarce resources; there are drives for autonomy among the various participating groups—who may be autonomous except for contractual relations—and there may well be divergence in subunit goals, unless the system manager continues to stress the paramount importance of the overriding goals or objectives of the entire system.

Pondy also found that competition can form the basis for latent conflict if the aggregated demands of participants for resources exceed the amount of resources available. Experience has shown that this is the most common type of latent conflict in system management.

The fact that efforts in system management continue to push forward the barriers of technology means that there is always a scarcity of well-trained people in the new technology. Consequently, there is competition for this scarce commodity. Pondy finds that autonomy needs form the basis of conflict when one party seeks to exercise control over some activity that another party regards as his or her own, or as his or her province, or seeks insulation from such control. This problem can be serious for the manager unless he or she takes great care to identify responsibility—and, just as important, accountability—for each activity in such detail that there is no chance of misperception about control by any party. In some cases, contractual coverage may be necessary clearly to define responsibilities. Pondy found that goal divergence is a source of conflict when the parties who must cooperate on some joint activity are unable to reach a consensus on concerted action. This problem, too, is a potentially serious one in system management and emphasizes the various factors involved in consensus decision making.

In the past, the system manager did not have sufficient authority to make decisions in all areas. He or she was dependent upon various co-ordinative devices—committees—through which to reach acceptable general agreement. The history of the dilution of technical objectives that resulted, however, has pointed up the necessity for allocating sufficient authority so that, once compulsory staff advice has been rendered, the system manager is authorized to make directive decisions. Pondy has also pointed out that two or more types of latent conflict may simultaneously be present. Experience shows that all three types of latent conflict exist in large and complex systems.

It is not possible to differentiate between those types of conflict that occur only vertically or only horizontally. Certain types—perhaps all —exist simultaneously. The discussion of horizontal conflict in the next chapter points out additional theory on conflict and underlines those areas where the system manager should apply attention to prevent conflict.

INTERFACE MANAGEMENT DEFINED

Interface management can be considered to have originated as a result of vertical conflict, as a result of horizontal conflict, or as a result of both. For purposes of the present discussion, there are advantages in considering it as both. The sorts of interfaces, which are encountered in system management and presented here, and the entire subject of interface conflict are expanded upon in the discussion of horizontal conflict in the next chapter. Chapter 6, on configuration management, also addresses interface management from both the technical and the behavioral points of view.

The Oxford Universal Dictionary, third edition, with corrections and revised addenda, 1955, does not list the word "interface." The *Encyclopedia Britannica,* 1973, defines an interface as "a surface separating two phases or states of matter, each of which may be solid, liquid or gaseous. An interface is not a geometrical surface but a thin layer that has properties differing from those of the bulk material on either side of the interface." *Webster's New Collegiate Dictionary,* 1974, states that an interface is "a surface forming a common boundary of two bodies, spaces or phases, or the place at which independent systems meet and act on or communicate with each other, as the man-machine interface, or broadly, an area in which diverse things interact or the means by which interaction or communication is effected at an interface."

Thus, the concept of interfaces and interface management was recognized or identified only a short while ago, and the search for a contemporary, authoritative definition continues. Meanwhile the concept of an interface as the place at which independent systems or interdependent systems, subsystems, organizations, groups, or individuals meet and act or interact on or communicate with each other is acceptable. The verb *interface,* of course, may be defined as the means by which such interaction or communication is effected at an interface. Interface management is then planning and control to achieve the common given objectives between the interaction of two or more groups.

Not all interfaces are aligned with system objectives. There may be social, political, economic, religious, moral, and so forth, interfaces that confront the system manager in addition to technical and behavioral ones; i.e., individual, group, and organizational interfaces that require much attention from the system manager. Not all interfaces come under the direct control of the system manager, and these may be the ones that prove to be highly difficult to manage. The system manager needs to identify those interfaces that do not come directly under his or her control and assign responsibility and accountability for them. The recognition of the interfaces and an awareness of the problems that may arise because of them will enable the system manager to prevent or counter such problems at an early stage. The importance of the numerous incidences of interface and the potential problems associated with them are difficult to overstate.

INTERPERSONAL AND INTERGROUP INTERFACES

If the system manager will but pause to contemplate, he or she will recognize that an interface exists between him or her and his or her deputy, assistant, executive assistant, or whatever other term is used for his or her alter ego and next in command. It is doubtful, however, that even the most tried and loyal deputy thinks in exactly the same way about every subject as the system manager does. The possibility of differences in points of view, and therefore of potential conflict, must be realized. There is certainly nothing wrong with differences in points of view. There are almost always a number of good ways to achieve a given objective, but the best way is almost always the one selected by the manager who is *accountable* for the achievement or nonachievement of the organization's objective. To have a subordinate who has good ideas and presents them clearly is perhaps for that very reason an asset to be desired.

The adept system manager quickly realizes that an interface exists between the system manager and whatever subordinate managers there are in the system-management office—the engineering manager, the configuration manager, the procurement and production manager. He or she similarly understands that there is an interface between the deputy or assistant or executive system manager and each subordinate manager. The number of interfaces grows astronomically as the interaction between lateral managers, subordinate managers, and their supervised personnel and between intergroup organizations and environments are considered. Certainly the number of interfaces increases at least in accordance with Graicunas's theory of span of control.[2] Although we must recognize that Graicunas's theory may not hold mathematical accuracy for each and every situation, it nevertheless serves to emphasize the possible problems in relationships that arise as the number of subordinates accountable to a given manager increases.

Intergroups may be perceived in a number of ways. The intergroup we are about to consider is the informal group that does not appear on organizational charts but is nonetheless an entity enjoying—or at least deserving—recognition as a body generating or reflecting interfaces. Such informal intergroup interfaces are important because of the fact that the evolution of their formation, development, and evaluation has been voluntary, and the odds are that the binding ties of the group were

---

2. V. A. Graicunas, "Relation in Organization," *Bulletin of the International Management Institute* (Geneva: International Labour Office, 1933), in Luther Gulick and Lyndall Urwick, eds., *Papers on the Science of Administration* (New York: Institute of Public Administration, 1937), pp. 181-187. Graicunas developed a mathematical formula indicating a geometric increase in complexities of management as the number of subordinates increases. Koontz and O'Donnell have demonstrated that whereas a manager with one subordinate has but 1 relationship, one with two subordinates has 6 possible relationships; one with four 44 possible relationships; one with five 100 possible relationships, and so on; until a manager with eighteen subordinates has a possible 2,239,602 relationships. (Harold Koontz and Cyril O'Donnell, *Principles of Management: An Analysis of Managerial Functions* (McGraw-Hill, New York, 1972), pp. 252-253.

developed not because of dedication to the achievement of organizational objectives but because of similar ethnic backgrounds, recreational interests, or other voluntary reasons.

ORGANIZATIONAL INTERFACES

There are at least two types of organizational interfaces—intraorganizational and interorganizational. Intraorganizational interfaces are under the control of the system manager, but interorganizational ones may or may not be. Usually at least some interorganizational interfaces represent those with organizations outside the system manager's control—as, for example, major contractors, subcontractors, and other lateral organizations with which no contractual responsibilities regarding interfaces were ever executed. (The importance and necessity of formal clarification regarding responsibility and accountability of specified interfaces has been more completely developed in Chapter 4.)

Organizational interfaces in the system-management office between, for example, the engineering organization and the configuration management organization, between the program-control organization and the procurement and production organization, and so forth, have already been identified. The point being underlined is that there are interfaces between each higher functional operation identified and shown on the organization chart. There may also be interfaces with the other major lateral organizations, autonomous in authority, over which the system manager has no control by way of delegated authority, but upon which he or she is dependent for effective achievement of system objectives; examples of the latter are the lateral divisions of a major corporation or lateral major commands in one of the military departments of the Department of Defense. For effective management, experience shows that the system manager must be delegated sufficient authority to control all interorganizational interfaces, if only through the assignment of a senior representative, executive, or manager of the lateral organization, accountable to the system manager, for the effective accomplishment of all interrelated tasks. Some system managers develop an organization to manage each interorganizational interface, staffed by representatives of each of the interfacing organizations, accountable to a single manager who executes performance ratings and has hiring and firing authority over each member of the interface management group. This manager is in turn accountable in every way to the system manager. Such an arrangement, which may require a contractual agreement between independent organizations, can be of great help in the effective pursuit of system objectives.

Figure 3.1 shows the identification of interfaces and their definition that occurs during the acquisition life cycle. It also shows some of the environmental factors that may affect the system management scheme. Environmental factors of a psychological, social, economic, political, technical, and religious or theological nature, plus even other environmental factors in certain cases, impact upon system management. The

FIG. 3.1:   ACQUISITION LIFE CYCLE SHOWING INTERFACES

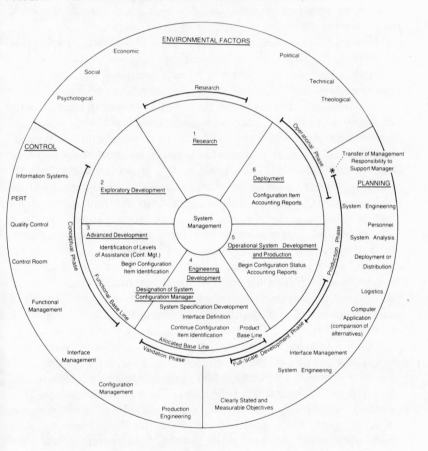

attention of the reader is particularly directed to the interfaces between the environmental areas and those between individuals, groups, and organizations whose primary interest lies within a single one of these areas.

Figure 3.1 also emphasizes the system manager's concern with the primary management functions of planning and control and their numerous interfaces. In the initial phase, the system manager makes plans for personnel and procedures in the system engineering area, conducts overall personnel planning and procedures, including plans for acquiring, training, supervising, motivating, and evaluating personnel for every functional and operating area of the entire system. Planning is accomplished for the system analysis function, the deployment or distribution function, the logistics function, for the utilization of computers and for the identification and control of each interface. The objectives in each operational area and at each hierarchical level should be clearly stated and measurable; that is, to have each objective stated in such a way that all concerned will know when it has been achieved is an invaluable tool.

Figure 3.1 depicts the variety of activities and interfaces that there are to control. Planning must be accomplished for the control phase, too. Control procedures are established in each functional area. The system manager plans for the accountability of subordinate managers to the system manager and, if necessary, plans for the contractual accountability of system participants outside the organizational line of authority of the system manager, for the type and utilization of information systems, including the determination·of what types of information are necessary and, equally important, what types of information are unnecessary. If PERT is to be used, detailed instructions issued to all concerned will aid understanding. Quality standards to assure compliance with specifications may be difficult to describe, but they are necessary. Control procedures established and implemented in each functional area measure progress toward objectives. Interface management procedures must be implemented, and strict control maintained. Configuration management procedures, due to their nature, must be strictly controlled. Plans are made, and control procedures implemented to assure the proper translation of design engineering and quality control documentation to production engineering personnel and to manufacturing, assembly, and test personnel.

Figure 3.1 shows that before the system has been formally identified as a system or possible system, sufficient pure, basic, and applied research has been undertaken to confirm that the proposed system offers reasonable promise of successful development. The potential system is then formally identified and enters the conceptual phase. The conceptual phase will probably require additional exploratory development, followed by advanced development, to assure that the system concept is technically feasible and cost effective, and to identify the preferable approach to the system objective. The functional base line is developed as one result of this phase.

Following completion of the conceptual phase, the system enters the validation phase. Engineering development is now accomplished, and early in this phase, the system configuration manager is designated. System specification also is developed; interfaces are defined; the configuration item identification continues; and the allocated base line is developed. The product base line is another important result of the validation phase. (Configuration management terms are defined and discussed in Chapter 6.)

If the results of the validation phase do, in fact, bear out the promise of the development of a successful system, the full-scale development phase may start even before the completion of the validation phase, resulting in some overlap. In the full-scale development phase, the operational system development is completed, and, a high probability of the achievement of a successful system being assured, production is begun, and so are configuration status accounting reports. With the production of operational units, deployment or distribution begins, and the system enters the operational phase. Configuration item accounting reports continue, and the management responsibility for the system is transferred to the support manager as early in the operational phase as a smooth transition will permit.

Thus, the job of a system manager is quite complex. He must see that all the foregoing activities are planned, staffed, controlled, and successfully completed within estimated cost and time schedules.

WHAT MAKES A GOOD INTERFACE?

In describing some characteristics of a good technical interface, Donald C. Loughry states that to provide an effective communication link, an interface system must offer flexibility, reasonable cost, and compatibility; in addition, an interface system should permit the interconnection of independently manufactured instrument and system components—whether from one or several manufacturers—so that all works as a single functional system. He further observes that a versatile interface must be compatible with at least five major categories of system components: measurement equipment, stimulus equipment, displays, storage units, and means of control.

The characteristics of a good management interface are similar to those of a good technical interface. The purpose of the management interface is to provide channels for the communication of information. Of primary importance are the recognition of the need for control, of the necessity for reducing to writing the objectives of the particular management interface, and how the objectives are to be achieved; that is, what procedures are to be followed and by whom. To provide a means of measurement, the objectives of the interface or its inputs and outputs must be stated in measurable terms. The stimulus equipment, or who is to provide the first transmission of information, must be identified, and some means devised to display the communication interaction occurring at the interface.

Any number of display methods are available to the system manager, from cathode-ray tubes to wall charts. Information storage units can be developed through logs of communications, tapes, files, reports of incidents, diaries, and minutes of meetings. The designation of an interface manager, accountable to the system manager, offers much to insure the implementation of control procedures. If these characteristics obtain, the interface will remain flexible, and the interface manager will be enabled actively to pursue this flexibility as an objective.

The cost of managing the interface is important. It is apparent that some interfaces must be maintained at any or all costs. The astute system manager determines ways to improve interface management while reducing the costs of the resources involved. Perhaps improved display methods may reduce the number of personnel required. The system manager assures that interface procedures, both technical and managerial, are compatible to all inputs, outputs, and participants.

The interface may represent the first consolidation of efforts of many hithertofore independent organizations—perhaps giant corporations or their divisions, smaller companies, or other autonomous divisions of the corporation producing the overall system. To insure compatibility, the system manager, through the interface manager, establishes planning meetings, so that all participants are aware of the objectives and of the required outputs, of what type and to what specifications. The fact that the interface manager is the accountable manager, and that inputs and outputs must conform to specifications must be made clear. Potential problem areas and the techniques to be employed to reduce the risk of problems arising should be pointed out. The interface manager is the team captain. He or she works to instill the idea that the interface represents a team effort, and makes sure that all those participating know the measurement techniques to be employed, the recourses to be followed in the event that input fails to meet specifications, and the appeal channels available for technical and behavioral problems. The necessity for a high degree of integrity in interface interactions should also be stressed. There is a need to develop in each participant the knowledge and confidence that everyone is working equally hard to achieve interface objectives and thus create an atmosphere of mutual trust.

The following steps to improve interface management are suggested:

1. Detailed identification of each interface
2. Statement of objectives of each interface
3. Assignment of responsibility and accountability for each interface

4. Delineation of the methods of communication at each interface

5. Insuring an understanding of interpersonal relations by all participants, stressing integrity, flexibility, intelligent cooperation, the expectation of differences in perception of roles, status, and interface relationships, and the development of team dedication to the reconciliation of viewpoints and progress toward achievement of objectives

6. Full exploration and knowledge of the interface, emphasis on the importance of the interface and of the role and contributions expected or demanded of each and every participant prior to the establishment of an interface management plan; theoretically speaking, this represents the coordination of thought during the planning phase

7. Recognition of information-transfer interfaces

8. Simplicity of inputs and displays

An additional suggestion calls for contractual coverage for the management of each interface. In the event that the interface manager is not under the organizational control of the system manager—i.e., if the interface manager normally belongs to another organization, another corporation, company, division, or military command, not under the direct line of authority of the system manager—the authority of the system manager is better recognized if provisions for the accountability of the interface manager to the system manager are spelled out.

4 ... ORGANIZATIONAL CONFLICT
A Horizontal Perspective

INTRODUCTION

Horizontal conflict may be defined as that effort expended by an individual, group, or organization in opposition to an individual, group, or organization participating laterally—or on the same level—in the development, production, and use of the same system. Whereas vertical conflict results from hierarchical problems of control and the delegation of power, horizontal conflict is caused by competition, communication, coordination, and the perceptions, skills, and characteristics of individuals, groups, and organizations.

The present discussion of horizontal conflict is based in large part upon the research of the team of Richard E. Walton and John M. Dutton and of that of Louis Pondy. The findings of these social scientists have contributed a great deal to the understanding of horizontal or lateral conflict—important knowledge for the system manager.

In their development of a model of interdepartmental or lateral conflict, Walton and Dutton established the following premises: (1) that the horizontal or lateral interactions in an organization are at least as important as the vertical interactions, and (2) that nine major types of antecedents can be described—mutual dependence, asymmetries, rewards, organizational differentiation, role dissatisfaction, ambiguities, common resources, communication obstacles, personal skills and traits.

Walton and Dutton also found that mutual task dependence is the key variable—task dependence being the extent to which two units depend upon each other for assistance, information, compliance, or other coordinative acts in the performance of their respective work. Overload conditions may intensify the problem of scarce resources and lead to bargaining; this may increase tension, frustration, and aggression and decrease the time available for social interactions that would enable the units to contain their conflict. High task interdependence and overload tend to heighten the intensity of either interunit antagonisms or interunit friendliness, increase the magnitude of the consequences of unit conflict for organization performance, and contribute to the difficulty of changing an ongoing pattern.

My own experience in the system management process has confirmed Walton and Dutton's findings. The system management process is filled with instances of task dependence with problems of mutual dependence upon scarce resources, and in the past, with the necessity of resorting to the bargaining process. Although that recourse has proved to be too costly in time, money, and the dilution of technical objectives to be effective in system management, it is nevertheless unlikely to disappear from human behavior. The incidence of high task interdependence and overload is frequent in the system management process. Many system managers therefore employ superordinate objectives, the development of an atmosphere of trust, and open lines of communication, all of which serve to eliminate or reduce interunit antagonisms. Most managers have found that to change an ongoing pattern requires an educational program on what change is required and why and how it is to be accomplished. Emphasis on superordinate objectives, progress reports, and open lines of communication are techniques that have proved effective.

Walton and Dutton have furthermore reported that symmetrical interdependence and symmetrical patterns of initiation between units promote collaboration, whereas asymmetrical interdependence leads to conflict. Conflict is also produced by differences in the way units are ranked along various dimensions or organizational status; namely, direction of initiation of action, prestige, power, and knowledge. When lower-status groups must direct higher-status groups even temporarily, the result is likely to be a breakdown in relationships between departments. Unfortunately, from the standpoint of asymmetrical interdependencies, the whole process of system management is filled with instances of imbalanced dependence upon certain functional specialties at varying periods of time. During the experience of a problem, many other functional groups will demand time from the analysis group. During the development and design phase, a number of functional groups may seek the expertise of the same, short-supply engineering specialty—for example, the assistance of the few experts in the magnetohydrodynamic area—at one and the same time.

Walton and Dutton found that interunit conflict results when each of the interdependent departments has responsibility for only one side of a dilemma embedded in organizational tasks. The more the evaluations and rewards of higher management emphasize the separate performance of each department, rather than their combined performance, the greater will be the conflict. Competition for rewards and recognition presents the same problems in system management as in any other management situation. The system manager, however, apparently has an advantage over other managers in this problem area because of the superordinate objectives of the system and the fact that the system manager can relate performance to cooperation.

According to Eugene Litwak, uniform tasks require a bureaucratic type of organization characterized by impersonality in human relationships, a prior detailed description of job policy and administration, and emphasis on general rules and specializations, whereas nonuniform tasks require a human-relations organization with contrasting characteristics. He observes that in contemporary society, most large-scale organizations have to deal with both uniform and nonuniform tasks, and must combine these contradictory forms of social relationships into a working professional model. Litwak has observed that the inclusion of these contradictory forms is a source of organizational conflict. His research thus reinforces Walton and Dutton's findings that organizational differentiation leads to conflict situations.

The whole process of system management, practically experienced, reinforces Litwak's findings. Although many tasks are nonuniform—one of a kind or first ever—many others are uniform, repetitive, routine. System managers have found that care in the selection process, opportunities for cross-training and promotion from within are effective techniques to reduce this type of organizational conflict.

Walton and Dutton point out that role dissatisfaction, stemming from a variety of sources, can be a cause of conflict. They cite examples where blocking status aspirations in functional areas or in staff members resulted in conflict, and they give other instances where professionals felt they lacked recognition and opportunities for advancement, a perception that almost invariably results in conflict. Whenever role dissatisfaction is present, Walton and Dutton found ambiguities in the definition of work responsibilities further increase the likelihood of interunit conflict.

Ambiguity also contributes to interunit conflict in several other ways. As an example, Walton and Dutton cite that difficulty in assigning credit or blame to one of two departments increases the likelihood of conflict between them. Another example is that low routinization and uncertainty of the means to goals increase the potential for interunit conflict.

The system manager is plagued with problems of ambiguity. To combat these problems he or she must share and give credit in the widest way. The clear definition of unit goals—showing how they contribute to the superordinate system goal—is another effective technique. Management-by-objective philosophy, whereby units as well as individuals participate in the establishment of objectives, stated in such a way that objectives can be used as standards of performance, is another proven tool to reduce ambiguity in performance criteria.

Walton and Dutton have found that potential conflict exists when two units depend upon a common pool of scarce organizational resources—such as physical space, equipment, manpower, operating funds, capital funds, central staff resources, and such centralized services as typing and drafting. If two units have interdependent tasks, the competition for scarce resources will tend to decrease interunit problem solving and coordinating. The message here for system managers is very clear. In system management, particularly when matrix management techniques are used, there are frequently dependencies of two or more groups upon a common pool of resources—in fact, each type of resource has been listed by Walton and Dutton. System managers have successfully used superordinate objectives where each unit contributes to the success of the other interdependent units. This technique, combined with performance evaluation based upon the amount of cooperation with other interdependent units, reduces the likelihood of conflict, and maintains a mutual problem-solving atmosphere.

Semantic difficulties, as Walton and Dutton reported, can impede communication processes that are essential for cooperation. Differences in training of personnel in various functional areas, such as contracting officers and engineers, also contribute to horizontal conflict. Organizational channeling of information introduces bias and hence conflict. On the other side of the coin, common experience reduces communication barriers and provides common referents. As one step in overcoming the semantic problem, system managers have found the publication of a system dictionary helpful, in order to insure that the terms commonly used have the same meaning to all personnel whatever the discipline and organization involved.

An overriding objective of the system might be the establishment of an open, trusting relationship between all those disciplines participating in system objectives. Some organizations are reputed to have employed the use of mirrors, conveniently placed, bearing beneath the mirror the admonition: "Here is how the organization appears to our customers." Another popular slogan is "Whatever we do, we can do better." Duplicate copies of this sort of communication can be dispensed to all functional groups at the same time to prevent allegations that information is distributed only in accordance with a priority list. All too often, recognition is given by a system manager in accordance with the opening statement "We did this . . ." or "We did that . . ." to advance the system objectives, rather than designating a specific unit for praise.

In regard to personal skills and traits, Walton and McKersie found that certain personality attributes, such as high authoritarianism, high dogmatism, and low self-esteem, increase conflict behavior. James D. Thompson has also stated that personal dissimilarities in background, moral values, education, age, and social patterns lower the probability of interpersonal rapport between unit representatives, and this, in turn, decreases the amount of collaboration between their respective units. Dutton and Walton also found that incongruities between departmental representatives in personal status—i.e., the degree in which they differed in rank, in various status dimensions, such as length of service, age, education, ethnicity, esteem in the eyes of superiors, pay, and so on—increase the chances for conflict. Personal satisfaction with the internal climate of one's own unit decreases the likelihood of a person's initiating interunit conflict. The lesson for the system manager from this research is that the development of an open, warm trusting climate is highly desirable. Superordinate objectives do much to reduce the effect of personal dissimilarities and personal status incongruities.

The project type of organization is frequently used in system management for short-term or special-effort endeavors. The research done by William R. Scott and Terence R. Mitchell indicates that probably the most important of all the distinctions between project and traditional structures is the project requirement that in the latter functions must be laterally and diagonally related. They find that such relationships accentuate forms of behavior which are minimized in conventional structures by reliance upon the chain of command as the primary means for obtaining coordination. Thus, the scalar indeterminacy that exists between project and department managers gives rise to a number of transactions that can only be described as political (Scott and Mitchell). Trading and bargaining, negotiation, conflict, and compromise are typical forms of behavior among executives engaged in working out lateral relationships. Through these relationships, executives attempt to achieve coordination among themselves—an activity that was formerly thought to be the function and the prerogative of hierarchy.

Early practical experience in system management would seem to corroborate Scott and Mitchell's findings. The dilution of system objectives, however, resulting from political transactions, became unacceptable, and the Department of Defense system management philosophy strengthened the system manager's position by increasing his authority to make directive decisions.

Long before the term "system management" was developed, Louis Pondy coined the term "system model" to deal with the problems arising out of the need for coordination. The use of Pondy's "system model" is not designed to confuse the reader but to remain consistent with Pondy's terminology. His system model, which was largely derived from the March-Simon treatment of organizational conflict, is appropriate for the analysis of conflicts among the parties to a functional relationship, since the system model is concerned with lateral conflicts, or conflicts among persons on the same hierarchical level.

The fundamental source of conflict in the system model arises out of the pressures toward suboptimization (Pondy). Important types of interdependence are the common usage of some shared service or facility, the sequences of a worker-information flow prescribed by task or hierarchy, and the rules of unanimity or consensus about joint activity (Pondy).

Practical experience in system management has reinforced Pondy's findings. In fact, the results of efforts to achieve consensus within lateral organizations were so poor in Department of Defense systems that the authority to make directive decisions was directly delegated to the Department of Defense system manager; efforts to achieve results through consensus decision led to conflict. As in most areas of study and research, not all studies of conflict and conflict management point in a single direction. My own thesis is that conflict is dysfunctional owing to the time and energy expended by those participants in opposition to one another, and to the scars that are left by conflict. Research buttressing this position is widely available, but so on the other hand, is research suggesting that conflict may serve a useful purpose. The very fact that some social scientists have found conflict useful means that their results deserve consideration. There must be some areas or instances where conflict, if very carefully controlled, serves a useful purpose. I myself would never recommend its use, however.

Most frequently the study of conflict has been motivated by a desire to resolve it and to minimize its deleterious effects on the psychological health of organizational participants and the efficiency of organization performance (Pondy). Robert L. Kahn and other researchers are of the opinion that one might well make a case for interpreting some conflict as essential to the continued development of mature and competent human beings. They found that the overriding bias of such reports is with the personal costs of excessive emotional strain, and report the fact that common reactions to conflict and its associated tensions are often both dysfunctional for the organization as an ongoing social system and personally self-defeating in the long run. Others state that some optimum level of conflict and associated personal stress and tension are necessary for progress and productivity, but portray conflict primarily as exacting a personal and social cost (Boulding). Still others feel that Elton Mayo, the Harvard social behaviorist noted for the Hawthorne studies, treated conflict too much as an evil, a symptom of management's lack in social skills, and its alleged opposite, cooperation, as symptomatic of health (Baritz). Practical experience in system management, however, has served to reinforce Elton Mayo's perception of conflict. Even as dispassionate a theory of organization as that propounded by James G. March and Herbert Simon defines conflict conceptually as a breakdown in the standard mechanisms of decision making; that is, as a malfunction in the system.

Pondy has observed that the two ways of reducing conflict in lateral relationships are (1) to reduce goal differentiation by modified incentive systems, or by proper procedures in selection, training, and assignment, and (2) to reduce functional interdependence. Functional interdependence can be lessened by reducing dependence on common resources, by loosening up schedules or introducing buffers, such as inventories or contingency funds, and by removing overpressure for consensus.

In applying the lessons learned from Pondy's research, the system manager might well reduce goal differentiation between lateral units by establishing superordinate objectives. Functional interdependence, however, is the way of life in system management. Practical experience has shown that educational programs to demonstrate the contributions of each functional group to the overall objective may well prove effective. The participants in system management are dependent on common resources— so a climate of cooperation is highly desirable. The pressure for consensus appears to exist in most groups. The system manager, however, usually abides by the principle of staff advice, hears all opinions, then makes whatever decision the group is to follow. The evaluation of performance based on cooperation is another suggestion to consider.

A common reaction to perceived conflict is the adoption of a joint-decision process characterized by bargaining rather than problem solving (Pondy). The system manager must be very careful, however, about the bargaining process! Some of the characteristics of the successful bargaining style have been described as careful rationing of information and its deliberate distortion; rigid, formal, and circumscribed interpersonal relations; suspicion, hostility, and disassociation among the subunits (Walton, Dutton, and Fitch). A danger flag is thus immediately raised for the system manager. In system management the channels of communication must always be open in both directions, and without the withholding of necessary information by senior echelons. The system-management process has always proved more successful when utilizing an open, trusting, warm, and informal atmosphere. The use of superordinate objectives, the evaluation of performance to include cooperation with interdependent managers and groups, and open active channels of communication have proved effective in eliminating suspicion, hostility, and disassociation among subunits. Pondy has observed that flexibility is a characteristic of a successful problem-solving relationship and that, conversely, a bargaining relationship is characterized by rigidity of demands and desires. Experience in the system-management process has reinforced this finding. As a result of seeking for consensus in the bargaining process, however, the system manager has been delegated the authority to make directive decisions, thus eliminating the earlier necessity of bargaining.

INTERFACE CONFLICT

A few years ago, the term "interface" was not to be found in the dictionary. The dictionary definition now is "the place at which independent systems meet and act on or communicate with each other." To make this definition more compatible with system management, substitute "interdependent" for "independent."

According to Paul R. Lawrence and Jay W. Lorsch, who have conducted much research and reported findings invaluable to system managers, interface conflict can best be managed when the attention devoted to interface management corresponds to the degree of differentiation between departments—in other words, the more dissimilarity there is, the more attention needs to be paid to the interface. The attention given to interface management in system management has grown to such proportions that in many instances the interface manager is contractually designated and his duties or tasks spelled out in detail. As we have already indicated, interfaces occur between the system manager and his or her deputy—or alter ego—between the system manager and his or her secretary, between the manager and his or her staff, between staff members, between functional subunits, and between every participating organization. Experience has shown the necessity of identifying the interface manager, specifying his or her duties, responsibilities, accountability, and designating communication channels.

Three factors promote effective resolution of interdepartmental conflict and thus high organizational performance (Lawrence and Lorsch): (1) a separate coordinating person or unit will be more effective if the degree of structure and goal, time, and interpersonal orientations of its staff personnel are intermediate between those of the units linked; (2) in resolving conflict, a separate coordinating unit will be more effective if its personnel has relatively high influence based on perceived expertise, and if units are evaluated and rewarded on overall performance measures embracing the activities of several departments; (3) interunit cooperation and overall organizational performance will be raised to the extent that managers openly confront differences, rather than smoothing them over or forcing decisions.

The designation of an interface manager serves to satisfy the requirements of Lawrence and Lorsch's findings. The interface manager may assume the role necessary to be perceived as an intermediate group between the units linked. The manager selected for each interface should have had the experience and record sufficient to show his or her expertise in conflict resolution. In fact, educational programs conducted by the interface manager in the identification and resolution of conflict problems may be used to enhance the manager's own qualifications and experience. Such programs may be utilized to air differences between groups, to confront differences—and to demonstrate which differences are not apt to be "smoothed over."

Some system managers find it desirable to apply interface management techniques at the configuration item level. To others, the existence of a configuration control board to consider and resolve changes—and their conflicts—is sufficient. Should an interface control committee be established, the inclusion of one member from each affected organization having the power to bind his or her group is recommended.

CONSEQUENCES OF INTERUNIT CONFLICT

According to Michael Crozier, the manifest characteristics of interunit conflict include a competitive orientation, bargaining and restrictions on information, circumscribed interaction patterns, and antagonistic feelings. Those managers who are unable to retaliate when conflict is initiated respond by withdrawing commitment to their jobs. John A. Seiler has reported that internal social stability, value sharing between units, and a hierarchy of legitimate interunit authority are important in whether interunit competition will or will not result in destructive conflict. Walton and Dutton have observed that it seems reasonable to assume that the more important the interdependences, the more a restriction on the interunit communication of information becomes damaging—as for example when a lateral relationship involves joint decision making, one unit can tip the decisions in its own favor if it alone has the controlling information relevant to these decisions; in such a case, minor concealment or distortion can be of great importance, particularly if the decisions being made are large ones. They report that channeling all interunit interactions through a few liaison persons in a conflict syndrome often reduces overall performance. The reason cited is that to ignore the contribution of those persons who are either affected by an internal decision or have potentially relevant information or opinions on the subject decreases the quality of the decision and lowers personal commitment to it. This tendency to avoid contact may result in implementation that lacks coordination. Horizontal conflict almost always involves stereotyping and encourages attitudes of low friendliness, low trust, and low respect—all good reasons why it should be prevented.

Walton and Dutton, in reporting on their research study of interdepartmental conflict, observed that competition in general results in motivation in some cases and in others debilitation. They also found that competition provides for checks and balances between units, that concealment and distortion of information lower the quality of decisons, that channeled interunit contacts enhance stability in the system, and that rigidity and formality in decision procedures enhance stability in the system but lower adaptability to change. Still other findings were that appeals to superiors for decisions provide more contact with superiors which may either increase or decrease the quality of the decisions; that a decreased rate of interunit interaction hinders coordination and implementation of tasks; and that distrust, suspicion, and hostility result in psychological strain, greater turnover in personnel, and decreased individual performance. In addition, the study established that poor performance, whatever its source, may lead to the very rewards, controls, and styles of supervision shown to be an antecedent to conflict. Higher executives who are dissatisfied with the performance of subordinate units frequently respond by reorganizing the units, with the result that feelings of status depreciation or power deprivation and the ambiguity that frequently follows such a reorganization only increase the potential for conflict. In sum, many researchers have found that if conflict arises in the traditional bureaucratic organization, it is likely to impede the coordinated pursuit of objectives, and practical experience in system management has reinforced their findings. (An appropriate question at this point might well be, Why is the bureaucratic organization of today so often described only as "traditional"? With all the theoretical and practical tools available to every system manager, there is every reason to believe that the bureaucratic model of organization of the present time—staffed by people of initiative and dedication, who are highly qualified for their positions, and have a high standard of fairness and moral values—can be an energetic and dynamic organizational model, able to both plan and control effectively to achieve organizational objectives.)

In Chapter 3, the fact that conflict occurs both vertically and horizontally was pointed out. In our conceptual consideration of conflict, we have considered some of the circumstances that lead to both vertical and horizontal conflict. Let us now briefly reconsider vertical conflict to show that those situations in hierarchical organizations that lead to vertical conflict have an effect on lateral conflict as well.

Claggett Smith has stated that conflict has the most significant consequences on those organizations that have a complex, differentiated structure with control centralized in the upper echelons. It should be emphasized that the entire process of system management is based upon a complex differentiated structure with control centralized in the upper echelons. Smith found effective leadership is an important variable in the prevention or resolution of conflict, and advance planning and coordination appear to be important in managing conflict generated by an over-bureaucratized form of organization. According to Smith, leadership may operate as a compensatory mechanism to offset problems of communication, organizational commitment, or differences of interests generated by a hierarchical form of organization. A pattern of high mutual influence among organizational members that crosses hierarchical levels and specialties may prevent destructive conflict. Arnold Tannenbaum has reported that this pattern of reciprocal influence is also apt to facilitate the development of a broader range of shared perceptions and attitudes among organizational members. Smith has also reported that the expansion in the control exercised by those lower in the hierarchy, tends to counteract the consequences of the hierarchical organization and serves to equalize, to some extent, the differences in status, authority, and organizational rewards that seem to play so significant a part in the development of conflict.

The lesson for the system manager here is that in working in an environment of a complex, differentiated structure, advance planning and effective leadership have been found to be important variables in the prevention and resolution of conflict. In addition, effective leadership is a compensatory factor that offsets problems in communication and encourages patterns of high mutual influence crossing vertical and horizontal organizational lines. To reiterate, Tannenbaum's finding that patterns of reciprocal influence are likely to aid in the development of shared perceptions and attitudes is important to the system manager in its emphasis on superordinate system objectives; Smith's finding that expansion of control by those lower in the hierarchy tending to offset differences in status, authority, and organizational rewards—factors significant in the development of conflict—is likewise meaningful in encouraging the system manager to permit to whatever extent reasonable, the expansion of control in the lower echelons to offset those factors that otherwise might encourage the development of conflict.

WHAT CONFLICT MEANS TO THE SYSTEM MANAGER

We have seen that conflict is to be expected in system management, as it is in any other organizational model that is a social system composed of human beings exhibiting the undesirable as well as the desirable characteristics of their kind. The fact that structural variables affect human behavior, and therefore, the possibility or probability of conflict, and that this possibility is enhanced or inhibited by interpersonal processes has already been emphasized. The value system of each individual, with each of its influencing factors, plays a vital role in these interpersonal processes.

The type and method of controlling mechanism—or mechanisms—and the judgment with which these control devices are applied has been shown to be a factor in the expectation and incidence of conflict, in system management as in other organizational models. The problems of communication, the size of the system organization, the diversity of specialties employed, and the roles that individuals or groups project are factors in the possibility of conflict. Such coordinating methods or devices—usually employed when the system manager does not have delegated or formal authority—as informal authority, functional authority, acceptance authority, or contractual authority with extraorganizational groups, may enhance or inhibit the probability of conflict. The fact that each group or organization in the system may perceive overall system objectives differently is another contributing factor. The perceptions of the authority of the system manager and each manager affected by other managers, both hierarchical and lateral, by contract or by influence, and by employees, likewise contribute to the possibility of conflict. The differences in basic motivations of employees and managers throughout the system, the pressure for and methods used to insure suboptimization, the perceived character of the overall system, as projected by the senior management, are all factors that affect the probability that conflict will arise. In the long run, the character of the system is a reflection or application of the personal value systems of senior management.

It is interesting to consider the numerous environmental and behavioral factors that contribute to the development of the personal value system of each individual. Some very interesting research has been conceptualized as a social system scheme. This conceptualization indicates how background factors—both external to the organization and internal—influence behavior and consequences. Anthony G. Athos and Robert E. Coffee define a leader as one who influences his followers to achieve an objective in a given situation, and point out that the manager has the right, as a function of his formal position and role, to direct or order people to behave so as to achieve objectives. The leader without any formal authority also influences people to behave so as to achieve objectives. Every effective manager is actually a leader as well as a manager, but it does not follow that all managers are leaders. The important distinction rests on the concept and use of authority. The manager may direct people only through the use of his or her formally delegated authority; the leader influences people through the use of personal power or informal authority. The effective manager does both.

From a practical standpoint, the system manager must often deal with subordinate managers, lateral managers, or interface managers who doubt the wisdom of the original plan that is being implemented. Although it is all very good and well to wish that the system manager will be able to influence them to comply voluntarily and enthusiastically with his directives, it is a fact of life that the system manager, as well as any other effective manager, must at times resort to the use of authority to direct people to behave so as to achieve given objectives. The system manager does not have the time, if, indeed, the inclination to convince by influence alone each doubting Thomas that the plan being implemented is the optimum. Conversely, it follows, of course, that conflict may arise if the affected manager is unwilling to subordinate his or her personal ambition and desire for self-aggrandizement to the efforts of the system manager to implement the approved plan.

There are numerous approaches or alternatives that can be taken to achieve specified objectives. The system manager should not be expected to convince, through influence, each newly installed project manager of the wisdom of the selected plan. This concept has been a controversial one in the past. I remember some years ago when I was doing some research on the Department of Defense, a senior staff member replied to one of my questions concerning the use of committees by system managers as a substitute for authority, "That is not the way it is." The point I am making is this: The staff, who wrote the policies for system managers—in this case—thought or perceived of the system manager as having sufficient authority to assure that lateral participants would follow the system manager's "desires." Yet at the same time, 54 percent—over half—of the system managers questioned reported having used at least one coordinative method as a substitute for authority. Fifty-seven percent of the system managers reported a belief that sufficient authority—delegated to them—could reduce acquisition costs.

Many results of conflict have been cited. This review has not attempted to place them in any order of importance, but the consequences certainly include a dilution in the strength and pursuit of system objectives, a diminution in the process of communications, limitations on personal freedom and the opportunity for personal growth, and the appearance of metaphorical walls enclosing spheres of influence. Conflict creates a hostile environment, reduces the desire and opportunity for innovation, constricts creativity, and develops a competitive orientation or environment. It results in the condition of having to bargain for information and restricts the flow of communication. Conflict develops antagonistic feelings, an environment of little or no trust, little or no respect for peers, superiors, or subordinates, and low friendliness for coworkers; it causes a lowered or lessened stability in the entire system, and imposes psychological strain on every participant. For the system manager, conflict is dysfunctional and costly; it should be avoided by planning to whatever degree possible.

RECOMMENDATIONS TO REDUCE THE PROBABILITY OF CONFLICT

Claggett Smith has observed that techniques of supportive leadership and the development of high mutual influence among lateral managers, which crosscut both specialist and organizational echelons, seem to provide a counterbalance to the strains induced by hierarchical organization (1966).

According to Gerald R. Miller, conflict can be temporarily averted or resolved if one of two disputants voluntarily submits to the will of the other. Arguments, he finds, are the rhetorical staple of persuasion; a person either wins or loses an argument. Miller further reports that if the two parties are not prepared to submit to verbal defeat, and if they possess no other ways to resolve the conflict, the breakdown of persuasion is inevitable. The lesson to be learned here by system managers is that discussions concerning alternatives should always be conducted on a professional level, and that the issues should remain professional. A functional manager must not be forced to become so closely associated personally with an alternative that he or she perceives the solution or selection as a win-or-lose situation. There is usually more than one viable alternative to a decision. The arguments—advantages and disadvantages—need to be presented professionally and discussed in an atmosphere of trust.

Although no universal panacea is known, the following numerous possibilities of ways to avoid conflict are offered for consideration. Researchers have identified a wide spectrum of leadership styles, from the authoritative, autocratic mode that allows no participation, usually characterized as the "no-trust" style, to the opposite extreme or style of laissez-faire or "hands off." The laissez-faire manager allows full participation by subordinates, who are able to enjoy the acceptance—or bottom-up—theory of authority in an atmosphere of full trust. The participative style of leadership lies midway in the spectrum with the use of authority by the manager being about evenly matched with the participation of subordinates. The style of leadership that a system manager uses should be a conscious choice, one that enables him to administer comfortably. Different styles of leadership are required for different situations and different individuals. The system manager should consciously develop patterns of mutual influence whereby he or she can exert influence in situations where he or she has no direct authority.

There may well be instances where the system manager perceives that he or she has insufficient authority. He or she must then resort to influence through leadership. The system manager has a better chance to develop patterns of reciprocal influence with those people who share similar perceptions concerning system objectives rather than with those who do not.

A study of the views of managers of large complex systems has shown that 45 percent of those answering reported that they, as system managers, had been forced to "sell" members of coordinative committees on the wisdom of their recommendations; 54 percent stated that they had to resort to committee decision making because they lacked sufficient authority to make and implement the decisions for all participants in the system (Lanford, 1965).

The system manager may also be faced with the task of clarifying the perception that subordinates exhibit in imputing superiority to supervisors. Supervisors are human beings also, and their superiority, if any, lies in the fact that through self-discipline and perseverence they have improved their technical and administrative skills. In areas of functional competence, the supervisor develops technical competence or surrounds himself or herself with a superb technical staff to insure that subordinates perceive that authority is administered by those managers who are technically highly qualified.

The successful system manager recognizes the right to privacy and personal dignity of all associates and employees. He or she develops a spirit of cooperation among all system participants, thus reducing the tendency of some to resort to methods of cutthroat competition or competitive practices to attract attention. All participants develop an understanding of the system objective, their group's objective, and exactly what contribution they are expected to make. The system manager realizes that not everyone who sees a chart perceives the same thing, understands words to mean the same thing, or conceptualizes a situation in the same way; he or she therefore tries to project the correct image and thus communicate with each person individually. The system manager clarifies the roles of specialists and hierarchical management and sees that they are understood by all participants so that they will be supportive of one another. Each hierarchical level and each group and subgroup have identifiable goals contributing to the overall system objective.

Probably the system manager's most important task is the selection of qualified managers, technical personnel, staff personnel, and working personnel. The subsequent training of managers and subordinates is another task to be faced. The system manager develops operating procedures that are easily understood, with a priority list, if necessary, where there is dependence of multiple groups on common resources. It is well to clarify all interface relationships in writing; as we have already mentioned, a written memorandum of understanding for all interface actions is highly recommended. Through repetition, each and every unit is made aware of its role and objectives and how each contributes to the overall scheme. The system manager works diligently toward a reduction of pressure through consensus decisions, relying on advice from technical experts.

The more abstract and dynamic the problems an organization absorbs, the greater part autocratic decisions must play, according to Adrian McDonough. The system manager so organizes his or her personal staff as to assign problems to the most qualified individuals or groups. It is not realistic to seek a consensus opinion or decision from individuals whose only qualification is the desire to be heard. In fact, in the research study mentioned earlier, 37 percent of those responding reported that the effort to achieve consensus among various coordinative committees advising the system manager had resulted in a compromise revision of system objectives (Lanford, 1965).

Other researchers in the area of large and complex systems have commented on the need for centralized authority and control and noted that methods for effecting this control need to be improved (Reckmeyer). Your attention is again directed to the highly successful implementation of centralized authority and improved control precedures in the Department of Defense system management offices.

Robert Katz has stated that to be effective an administrator needs three basic personal skills—the technical, the human, and the conceptual. The administrator must have (1) sufficient technical skill to accomplish the mechanics of the particular job for which he or she is responsible, (2) sufficient human skill in working with others to be an effective group member and to be able to build cooperative effort within the team he or she leads, (3) sufficient conceptual skill to recognize the interrelationships of the various factors involved in his or her situation, which will lead him or her to take that action which is likely to achieve the maximum good for the total organization.

Katz's three necessary administrative skills appear like a golden rule for success in system management. As mentioned earlier, Claggett Smith also found that effective leadership seems to be an important variable in the prevention or resolution of conflict, and that advanced planning and co-ordination are important in managing conflict occurring in an overbureau-cratic form of organization (1966). He also stated that a pattern of high mutual influence among organizational members which crosses hierarchical levels and specialties may prevent destructive conflict, or it may help to manage it once it has arisen. Smith suggested that this pattern of control may be effective partly because of better communication and inter-personal relationships, allowing a more flexible way of resolving conflicts.

The system manager, then, should possess conceptual skill in order to understand the primacy of the organization's objectives and to be able to perceive which subordinate or peer manager is not working harmoniously toward system objectives. Training programs for managers in the im-portance of interfaces, styles of leadership, development of communica-tions, and an identification and appreciation of the primacy of system objectives have proved to be effective management development tech-niques in the past.

Robert R. Blake and Jane Srygley Mouton have developed an effective tool for use in the resolution of conflict. They describe it as the "Fifth Achievement"—a sharply increased understanding by everyone of the roots of conflict and the human skills to gain the resolution of differences (1970). The fifth achievement is the establishment of a problem-solving society where differences are subject to resolution through insights that permit the protagonists themselves to identify and implement solutions to their differences upon the basis of committed agreement. The hoped-for achievement of the future is that ultimately men and women will be able to work out, face to face, their differences.

Blake and Mouton have also developed a conceptual basis for analyzing situations of conflict. Their Conflict Grid® is a way of identi-fying basic assumptions about how human beings act in situations where differences are present, whether the disagreement is openly expressed or silently present (1970). This conceptualization is shown in Figure 4.1.

Your attention is directed to the five positions shown in the Conflict Grid®. In the lower left-hand corner, position 1-1. neutrality is being maintained at all costs. In position 9-1, at the lower right-hand corner, conflict is suppressed through the authority-obedience approach. In position 1-9, at the upper left-hand corner, disagreements are smoothed over or ignored, so that surface harmony is maintained. Position 5-5, in the center, represents compromise, bargaining, and middle-ground positions. Position 9-9, at the top right-hand corner, conceptualizes the situation where valid problem solving takes place with varying points of view objectively evaluated against facts and emotions.

To underscore the point once again, note that in Figure 4.1, the 5-5 position is that of settling disagreement through bargaining, a compromise solution. This stance means agreeing for the sake of being agreeable, even to the point of sacrificing sound action—in other words, settling for what you can get, rather than working to get what is sound in the light of the best available facts and data. (Earlier research into system management techniques by Reckmeyer (1958) and Lanford (1965) corroborate these findings.)

FIG. 4.1:   THE CONFLICT GRID FIGURE

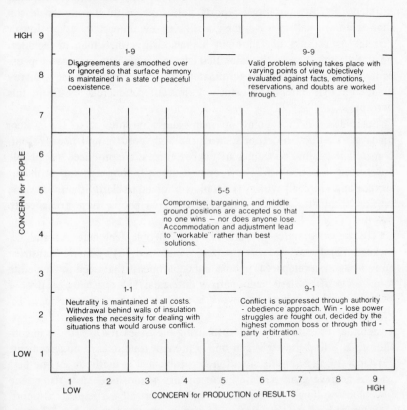

Source: "The Fifth Achievement" by Robert R. Blake and Jane Srygley Mouton. "Journal of Applied Behavioral Science," 6 (4), 1970, p. 418. Reproduced by permission.

The 9-9 position of Blake and Mouton's Conflict Grid® represents a foundation of interdependence that can be a strong basis for an open, problem-solving society in which men and women can have and express differences of opinion and yet be interrelated in ways that promote the mutual respect, common goals, and trust and understanding all must have to achieve results in ways that lead to personal gratification and maturity. Blake and Mouton reported that if the "Fifth Achievement" is to be realized, greater use of the behavioral sciences seems essential, so that men and women can share and evaluate their differences, learn from them, and use conflict as a stepping-stone to the greater progress that is possible only when differences can be resolved in a direct, face-to-face way (1970).

Warren H. Schmidt has found that the typical manager is likely to spend about 20 percent of his or her time dealing with some kind of conflict, either as a participant or as a mediator, helping others to resolve their differences. Other published reports state that the most common reason that senior managers leave their positions—by requested resignation or "firing"—is because of failure in human skills rather than in technical ones. Still other research states that about 80 percent of those top executives "terminated" were terminated for lack of human skill. A survey made through interviews which I myself conducted confirms this percentage.

Schmidt's findings point up many areas of interest to the system manager. Conflict, he reports, produces both positive and negative outcomes. The positive outcomes are (1) better ideas are produced; (2) people are forced to search for new approaches; (3) long-standing problems surface and are dealt with; (4) people are forced to clarify their views; (5) tension stimulates interest and creativity; (6) people have a chance to test their capabilities.

The negative outcomes are (1) some people feel defeated and demeaned; (2) distance between people is increased; (3) a climate of distrust and suspicion develops; (4) people and departments that need to cooperate look only after their own narrow interests; (5) resistance—active or passive—develops where teamwork is needed; (6) some people leave because of the turmoil.

Schmidt finds that, in conceptualizing the issues at stake, those in conflict usually find themselves in one or more of four areas of disagreement: (1) facts—or the present situation or problem; (2) methods—or the best way to achieve goals; (3) how participants would like things to be; and (4) values or long-term goals and qualities that all participants support.

Schmidt reports that, after identifying the nature of the difference between conflicting parties, it is useful to ask, "What might be the reason for this difference?" Among the most common reasons are (1) informational, that is, the parties are exposed to different information; (2) perceptual, or different interpretations of data; and (3) role, that is, role expectation that require different positions e.g., management versus labor.

Schmidt has also developed a conceptualization of ways to handle conflict, which is shown in Figure 4.2.

FIG. 4.2:   WAYS OF HANDLING CONFLICT

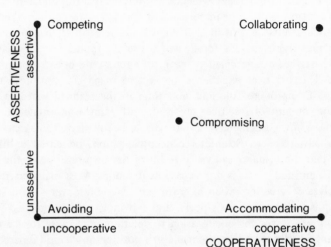

Source: "Conflict, A Powerful Process For (Good or Bad) Change," Warren H. Schmidt, "Management Review," December 1974, © 1974 by AMACOM, a division of American Management Associations. All rights reserved. Reprinted by permission of the publisher.

The explanation of the figure is as follows: The position in the upper left-hand corner is that of Competing, which involves going all out to win your objectives at the other's expense. Placed opposite—in the lower right-hand corner—is Accommodating, which means neglecting your own concerns to let the other person achieve what is important to him or her. Avoiding a confrontation makes sense when there seems little chance to resolve the conflict in a satisfactory way because the timing is wrong or the issue is not sufficiently critical. The position in the center of the figure is that of Compromising; that is, settling for half a loaf rather than risking an all-out, win-or-lose struggle. The position in the upper right-hand corner is that of Collaborating, which is a kind of mutual problem solving. Each person accepts the other's goals, and they work together to achieve the best for both. Instead of dividing the pie, they seek ways to make the pie bigger. The position in the lower left-hand corner of the figure is that of Avoiding Conflict—even at the expense of progress toward the achievement of organizational goals.

Schmidt underlines the fact that before conflict can be managed, it must be understood. Part of the management of conflict involves making a conscious choice of which is the best method to use, and knowing why it seems best in a given situation. Conflict can be handled more creatively and effectively when it is viewed not as a process to be feared and suppressed but as one to be understood and managed.

The weight of empirical evidence certainly seems to point out clearly to the system manager the importance of understanding conflict, the need for conscious involvement in it, including concrete situations, an analysis of the underlying reasons for it, and a studied application of whatever method has been ascertained to be most appropriate in each specific instance. The practical experience of system managers reinforces these findings. Compromise solutions add time to the planned schedule, and with the amount of resources involved, both human and material, it is easy to see how costs rapidly escalate when schedules have to be extended.

The advantage to Schmidt's conceptualization, presented in Figure 4.2, is that the manager can visualize his or her own position on the grid, though admittedly this is not as easy as it sounds. Most managers regard themselves as superior, when in truth most are about average. Questionnaires, discussion with one's peers, and exit interviews—conducted when an employee leaves the organization to determine the cause for leaving—can bring insight as to how the manager's position on the grid is perceived by others. Once the manager has determined his or her position, the next step is to decide where on the conceptual grid he or she wants to be. To assist him in moving to his desired position there is an ever-increasing amount of theory to assist him. Behavioral or organizational behavior theory will prove of real assistance.

5 . . . THE SYSTEM MANAGEMENT OFFICE

INTRODUCTION

In Chapter 2, we examined the bureaucratic organization and determined that it can be effectively used to manage large and complex systems as well as smaller ones. We shall now examine in some detail the functions of a typical system-management office.

Ever since the days of Aristotle, there have been continous efforts made to develop a unified theory of knowledge. Present-day efforts appear to have begun in 1928 with Ludwig von Bertalanffy's proposal to develop a general system theory. Although his theory was proposed as an explanation of the interactions of biological systems or organisms, other researchers have attempted to develop and apply a general system theory to show the relationships between all fields of science and thus unify the entire empirical world of knowledge. General system theory was developed around the concept of the whole—in opposition to those earlier practices, advocated by Descartes, of analysis, or breaking down an organic whole into its most elemental parts for examination. General system theory attempts to deal with organized complexity and with the interactions and interrelationships between numerous parts, which are often but loosely associated. Its long-range goal, as we have indicated, is to unify all science through the development of mathematical concepts and terminology. Short-term application includes the development of models to indicate relationships and to highlight the interfaces between disciplines. The utility of the general system theory is as a conceptual framework or device that sets forth the component parts, showing the relationships perceived, the interfaces, the various factors—background, environmental, economic, social, and technological—and the importance in the whole scheme of values and value judgments. Such a framework assists the system manager in understanding the many complexities involved in present-day systems and in achieving predetermined objectives. The component parts, the relationships perceived, the interfaces, and the various factors involved may then be subjected to as penetrating an analysis as the system manager desires. Thus, general system theory and the methods of analysis formulated by Descartes and Galileo are not to be considered as incompatible but rather as reinforcing each other. The theory is useful in the analysis of component parts of a system and in the conceptual reconstruction, reassembly, or synthesis of the parts into the whole, with its synergistic effect. General system theory is a method of insuring consideration of factors that have previously been considered unimportant, not pertinent, or simply overlooked.

A system approach focuses upon the formulation of a set of objectives —ends to be achieved by solving specific problems—a formulation that is derived through an analysis of the operational or marketable system to be supported. There are constraints that must be considered, parameters within which solutions to problems must fall, and limitations on resources. The system approach does not interpret constraints as an excuse for mediocrity, but responds to these constraints by organizing the available technology, manpower, economic and other resources, so as to reach within a specified time frame, predetermined objectives. The system approach, in other words, is a management tool that plans and controls the actions required for cost-effective achievement of specified objectives.

SYSTEM MANAGEMENT DEFINED

System management, as we have already indicated, is concerned with the planning and managing of the technical, business, and human resources in a particular cycle. This includes the planning and control of the initial or definition phase, development phase, and production phase of the system. It also includes the assurance that planning is being accomplished by those subsidiary organizations responsible for the complementary functions of logistics and maintenance support, personnel training, operational training, activation of user organizations, and the deployment of the system—its personnel, hardware or software, and support resources.

A system may be defined as an ordering of environmental factors— human, financial, and material; methodologies, such as cybernetics, computer application, communication theory; the social system conceptual scheme; management philosophy and leadership to achieve a predetermined objective. System management, then, is the planning and control of the components of the system to achieve the system objective.

Forecasts of the behavior of environmental factors thus become premises for the long-range planning function of the system manager. This emphasizes the importance of the interfaces between individuals, groups, organizations, their disciplines and philosophies. An interface, as we have seen, has been defined as the point of contact between individuals, both laterally and vertically, and between groups, organizations, disciplines, and philosophies.

Figure 5.1 shows the relationships of system management, system analysis, and system engineering.

FIG. 5.1: RELATIONSHIPS OF SYSTEM MANAGEMENT, SYSTEM ANALYSIS, SYSTEM ENGINEERING

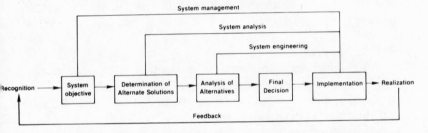

It reinforces the observation that system management provides a conceptual framework. The system approach is, in effect, a particular strategy or set of attitudes for approaching the management task. System analysis and system engineering are managerial tools or techniques useful in designing a new system, improving an existing system, or solving a specific situational problem.

SYSTEM ANALYSIS

David Cleland describes system analysis as any orderly analytic study designed to help a decision maker select the preferred course of action from among possible alternatives. He says that it represents an approach to, or way of looking at, any complex problem of choice under conditions of uncertainty. He also states that the entire system concept is far more widely discussed than understood.

The very terms "system management," "system analysis," and "system engineering" sometimes cause confusion, and have, perhaps, contributed to the lack of understanding of the system concept. One definition of system management is the planning and control of the component subsystems, resources, and interfaces in the system to achieve the system objectives. System analaysis is usually considered a subfunction of the planning function and is the examination of alternative courses of action to achieve the objective, or the development of additional alternatives when required. Quantitative techniques are used to the maximum degree in the development and comparison of alternative courses of action, but not necessarily exclusively. Where quantitative data are not available, the system analyst must develop qualitative subjective judgment data. Then the system manager must use qualitative subjective judgment in making his or her decision of choice among or between alternatives.

The process of system analysis involves the collection of data that provides information about the system and its operation. Analysis of this data should produce a series of statements that describe the system in terms of

1. Its objectives and/or purpose
2. The functions of performance required to satisfy the objectives
3. Human functional responsibilities, i.e., the human-system relationship
4. Major subsystems and components used to structure the system
5. Equipment or materials required
6. Established concepts, policies, or procedures required for operation, maintenance, or utilization
7. Effects of environmental factors on system operation and maintenance
8. Systematic examination of alternatives
9. Comparison of alternatives
10. Consideration of uncertainty.

SYSTEM ENGINEERING

Frank Jankowski, in an unpublished paper, defines system engineering as devoted to the optimum selection, specification, and use of engineering organizations, processes, inventory, materials, and economic resources to accomplish a defined task.

To the system manager then, system engineering refers to engineering management efforts to direct and control a totally integrated engineering effort, including system engineering, design engineering, support engineering, production engineering, and such specialty fields as reliability, maintainability, system effectiveness, safety and human factors. System engineering is the application of scientific and engineering effort (1) to transform a requirement or need into an appropriate functional description and system delineation and configuration through the use of an iterative process of definition, synthesis, analysis, design, test, and evaluation; (2) to integrate related technical functions and assure compatibility of all physical, functional, and program interfaces; and (3) to incorporate such special technical efforts as reliability, maintainability, safety, human factors, and other such factors into the total engineering effort.

FIG. 5.2: **A COMPARISON OF THE FUNCTIONS OF SYSTEM MANAGEMENT, SYSTEM ANALYSIS, & SYSTEM ENGINEERING**

	System Management	System Analysis	System Engineering
Framework	conceptual	logic/reasoned	structured
Nature	total systems	analytical	developmental
Orientation	macro	evaluative	task
Emphasis	decision-making	problem solving	design & implementation
Methodology	integrative	analytic	engineering
Operating Level	management	staff	line
Approach	eclectic	scientific & iterative	practical
Application Level	broad	situational & ad hoc	particularized
Training	business	management-science	engineering
Skills	management	conceptual	technical

Source: R. A. Lancaster, unpublished paper in Graduate System Management Course, Wright State University, Dayton, Ohio 1976.

Figure 5.2 compares the terms "system management," "system analysis," and "system engineering." It shows that system management relates to the total decision-making process, system analysis emphasizes scientific inquiry and problem solving, and system engineering is developmental in nature and task-oriented, seeking utility of purpose and design.

System engineering is an orderly, structured approach to the marshaling of science and engineering knowledge to achieve practical technical objectives. It is concerned with the system parameters, the determination of performance inputs and outputs of each subsystem and component, and the integrated performance of the subsystems and components as an operating whole. As such, it is a process that can be compared to an iceberg, the system parameters comprising the tip, and the subsystem parameters, the submerged portion. The system manager, as well as the responsible system engineer, is ever conscious that the effectiveness of the entire system is the product of the effectiveness probability of Subsystem 1 times the effectiveness probability of Subsystem 2 times the effectiveness probability of Subsystem 3, and so forth. Mathematically stated, if the effectiveness probability or reliability of each of four major subsystems is .9, the system effectveness is .9 x .9 x .9 x .9 or .6561—usually an unacceptable level of system effectiveness or reliability.

Should the system manager decide upon a matrix organization, the accountability of each person moved from a functional area to an area of direct support to the system manager is usually spelled out, so that each manager enjoys full authority and the expectation of accountability over each person regardless of his or her functional allegiance. This —no matter what the time duration of the assignment—will assist each manager to achieve the objectives established for his or her area of work.

Figure 5.3 is a conceptualization of the system management scheme, showing the two major functions—planning and controlling—influenced by a number of environmental factors. The emphasis in planning is on clearly stated and measurable objectives, the emphasis in controlling is on standards of performance. An inspection of the environmental factors shows the importance of economic, social, political, and general technical considerations. There may be even more environmental factors that have an impact on a particular system; for example, psychological factors or perhaps even religious ones.

The system manager involved in system planning finds numerous factors to consider: system analysis, computer application, system engineering, preparation for interface management, provision and training of personnel, organization for system management, the definition of relationships for interrelated and interacting organizations, the training and deployment of user personnel, logistic support for the system, deployment or distribution of the system, and highly important, the authority-accountability-responsibility relationships of every individual, group, and organization involved in the development, production, and utiilization of the system.

A system is composed of a very large number of components: the end items to be used—aircraft perhaps, or an automobile, a refrigerator, a dam, the technical data or instructions needed for the use and maintenance of the end item; supply procedures and spare parts prepositioned in areas to meet anticipated needs; maintenance instructions, procedures, equipment, and trained personnel to maintain the end item; training facilities, procedures, and personnel if the use of the end item requires an experienced operator, with special skills, as a pilot; the necessary test

FIG. 5.3: THE SYSTEM MANAGEMENT SCHEME

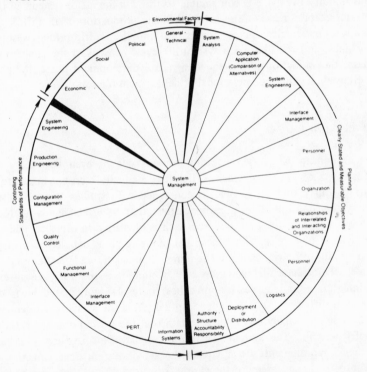

and check-out equipment, or other adjunct equipment, to service and maintain the end item; and the facilities to develop, test, manufacture, store, and maintain the end item. The system concept is to design, produce, use, and manage the system as an integrated unit, not as a series of individual efforts.

THE SYSTEM LIFE CYCLE

The military departments in the Department of Defense have for more than thirty years been developing concepts and implementing procedures for large, complex, and expensive weapon systems. The United States Air Force, for both conceptual and practical reasons, perceives the life cycle of a major system to extend over a period of six to eleven years and even longer, particularly if the system is a highly successful one and enjoys a long period of operational use—the B-52 aircraft, for example. This military life cycle is comparable to those in the major systems of the private sector, such as those involved in the production of aircraft, high-speed trains, nuclear power plants, automobiles, refrigerators, washing machines, and the like. Each system life cycle consists of the conceptual phase, the validation phase, the design and development phase, the production phase, and the operational or deployment phase.

CONCEPTUAL PHASE

The conceptual phase, requiring perhaps one or even two years of effort by a system management office that gradually increases in size to a staff of thirty or forty people, is concerned with studies to insure that the system concept is technically feasible, that its effectiveness justifies its cost, and that the preferred approach is identified in order to achieve the system objectives. The conceptual phase requires detailed identification of all technical concepts, required manpower, and facilities in all phases. This phase highlights any new technologies requiring design experimentation and suggests approaches to resolve anticipated areas of technical difficulty. During the conceptual phase the system management office conducts analyses to make certain that the system concept is technically feasible. The system manager is usually asked to show that the technical requirements do not push the art of system management too far into too many areas of the various subsystems, and that elements of costs have been recognized. The system management office confirms that cost estimates are complete and reasonable and that each area of technical risk has been identified, assessed, and found reasonable. During this phase, trade studies or trade-off analyses are conducted to determine which of perhaps a dozen approaches (or combination of approaches) is most desirable. The conceptual phase results in the development of a functional base line for the system and its subsystems, in an overall assessment of the risk involved, and if the risk assessment is acceptable, in an overall management plan to guide the system development through the succeeding phases of validation, full-scale development, production, deployment, and operational use. The conceptual phase identifies the items or subsystems requiring a long lead time to process through research, development, manufacturing, and testing.

VALIDATION PHASE

The validation phase requires perhaps one year of effort; and during it, the system management office may grow from a staff of thirty or forty persons to one numbering perhaps two hundred for a major system—some seventy-five for a less complex one.

During this phase, the system specifications are developed, and the system management office prepares a statement of work in order to collect bids from qualified contractors. The request for proposals precedes the development of the statement of work in instances where inputs or suggestions are desired from potential contractors—even if these are other divisions of the same organization—in order better to define the statement of work. Once bids have been submitted, the system management office selects the desired contractor or contractors. In very large and complex systems, this procedure often involves two steps or phases, the first phase being designed to obtain assistance from more than one contractor in the development of more specific system performance requirements and cost estimates. A rigorous study of design concepts and performance is necessary to determine which proposal is most desirable. The system management office is responsible and should be accountable for acquiring the system it envisions and desires, not the system some other participant thinks the system management office should have. The consideration of design concepts serves to highlight interfaces and provides leads as to what action is needed to clarify interfaces and to make provisions, contractually if necessary, for managers of major interfaces.

In the development of major systems in the private sector, the parent organization or corporation of the system manager may also be the parent organization of the group that is to develop and manufacture the system. In such an event, both the responsibilities and the authority of the system manager and his associates in the system management office must be recognized and accepted by every participant. When the further development and manufacture of the system are to be conducted by a contractor, the authority of the system manager and the system management office is frequently specified contractually. Technical exchanges between the system management office and the research, the design, the production, and the test engineers help to insure that the philosophy of the system manager and his management office remains the guiding dicta of the system.

In instances of prototypal development, the selection of contractors for later development and manufacture is also made in the validation phase. Competitive tests are conducted, analyses of the results are made, and the most desirable model selected. Afterward, the system management office prepares a request for proposals for full-scale development from the selected source. The system management office next develops the program management plan, which develops in detail the conceptual plan for management in each subsequent phase of the system.

DESIGN AND DEVELOPMENT PHASE

This is a highly busy phase. The system specification—a set of specifications describing the entire system and subsystems in detail—must be developed. The system management office then prepares a configuration item specification—a detailed description of all the hardware items in the system. A general specification which defines the design-engineering parameters of the system and its subsystems should also be made during this period.

Once the more comprehensive specifications have been completed, the detailed design specifications may be prepared and engineering drawings developed for use in the fabrication of developmental hardware. Continuing design reviews will probably prove necessary. A formal design review is accomplished as a commitment to accept the final design. The hardware configuration is determined by the initial specifications, preliminary drawings, and other technical data necessary to describe the functional base line. Any subsequent changes in the hardware configuration—and there will be many—are subject to formal control and follow an engineering route of change. The reason for this procedure is to make sure that all subsequent items are similar, that supply and maintenance requirements have been met, that needed changes in technical data have been accomplished, and to attempt to hold in some degree engineering changes to a minimum—which is not to be construed that necessary changes will be avoided.

The full-scale development phase may last as long as two or three years. During this time, the size of the system management office may reach 275 people for major systems or to some 130 for less complex operations. A system and subsystem fabrication and testing program to prove out the final system design objectives and configuration is conducted during the validation phase. Detailed design specifications are now finalized, and engineering drawings prepared, which become the basis for contracting for the desired operational qualities of the system. Next hardware design and development for test programs is begun, as are the tasks of planning for support equipment of all types—for logistic management, for personnel and training. During the final period of this phase, the formal procedures and techniques developed in the system-management office are put into operation. The functions of system engineering, configuration management, contracting, cost control, and all other measures of system management control are implemented. Initial operational testing is begun, and the evaluation of hardware and support equipment is also conducted.

PRODUCTION PHASE

This phase, lasting for a period of from two to five years, sees the system management office begin to decline in size, dropping back by the end of the time to some 150 people for major systems or to some 50 or 55 for those less large in size.

A study of the manpower requirement curve for system management that I once undertook proved highly interesting. In the early years of system management, the United States Air Force followed what at least at first appeared to be the "expected" manpower requirement curve; that is, a relatively small group in the system management office until the production phase, a build-up during the production phase, and a relatively steep decline in manpower requirements as the system starts to make the transition from the production to the deployment phase. The searching study of system management office manpower requirements, which was conducted in 1964-1965, showed, however, that manpower requirements increase rapidly as the system leaves the conceptual phase, continue to increase through the validation phase, and reach a peak late in the full-scale development phase. (These findings were a surprise; previously it was believed that the peak manpower requirements were during the production phase—see above.) Then, barring unforeseen or unexpected problems of a major nature, the size of the system management office begins to decline soon after the start of the production phase, dropping to perhaps half the strength at the end of the phase than was required at the entry into it. During the operational or deployment phase, the manpower requirements continue to drop, approaching zero or a merely housekeeping status, as the now successful system enjoys a long and productive service life.

During the production phase, the system is committed to production. Necessary contractual arrangements are made to insure complete understanding of what is desired and what is to be provided, and by whom and under what conditions. The production engineering task is now complete, and the logistic support activities are implemented. If called for, subcontracting arrangements are processed, and the physical configuration of the system hardware and its subsystems is finalized. In seeming repetition, after the configuration determination, all changes must once again be handled formally to insure uniformity in maintenance, supply, data, and training support. If responsibility for the management of the system is to be shifted upon completion of the production phase—as the military services transfer management responsibility from the acquisition office to the logistic support office—the transition should be made in accordance with previously prepared plans. The transfer of responsibility to the logistic support office is a major point in the system life cycle. To insure continuity, many logistic support managers place personnel in the system management office for some months prior to the actual transfer.

OPERATIONAL PHASE

The operational, or deployment, phase often covers a very considerable period of time. Note, for example, the length of life of the B-52 aircraft.

Early in the operational phase, management responsibility is usually transferred to the logistic support office. The logistic management office becomes the system management office, accepting responsibility for all documentation activities in the areas of budgeting for modifications or updating, for scheduling, for configuration management, for management of all technical data, supply contracts, maintenance requirements, engineering responsibility, and continuing test procedures.

We have seen that a system is the sum of its parts, a complete entity that is intended to fulfill an operational role. This means that for a system to be successful, it must be developed with an awareness of the operating environment and that this environment must now include a consideration of economic, political, and social factors as well as technological and physical ones. In the operational phase, the environment no longer consists only of temperature ranges for operation, expected mean temperatures of various operating locations, hours per day of expected operation, and various technical parameters. The impact of political action, of social acceptance or possible nonacceptance, of economic conditions, of possible religious ramifications, psychological ramifications, and of others that the system manager and his staff can envision, must be considered.

SYSTEM DOCUMENTATION

Documentation of all system activities is an inglorious, detailed, nagging, but necessary part of system management activities. Doubtless the reader will recall the anecdote of the Airborne missile that was finally launched successfully, but that could not be duplicated because no formal record of all the changes made in it had been kept.

Another similar anecdote is about the attempts of a customer to reorder an item previously purchased. Basically, the item looked like a fifty-five-gallon oil drum (priceless at today's prices), filled with cement, or some substance similar to the characteristics of cement, but with the center of gravity very precisely located. Indeed the precise location of the center of gravity in this item was the paramount specification. A solicitation of bids was made, and the lowest bidder was, of course, selected. The successful bidder, not realizing the difficulty of precisely locating the center of gravity, delivered an item that did not fulfill this requirement. The original manufacturer was then asked to provide drawings, which he did. Bids were then asked for in conformance with the previous specifications, and copies of the drawings were attached. The low bidder was again accepted, and again, the delivered item was useless because the center of gravity was again imprecisely located. Investigation revealed that the successful bidder could not "read" the drawings provided because the original draftsman had failed to include some processes or steps which it was necessary to follow in order to get the real meaning of the drawing. The point being made is that the system manager cannot *assume* that formal records of all actions are being maintained. The development and maintenance of documentation is vital to the health of the system.

A major system is developed to fulfill a requirement that may be an economic or competitive opportunity or to counter a perceived economic or competitive threat. The objective—whether opportunity or threat—is normally set down in writing; that is, the parameters of the desired system are clearly specified. An early step is the development of a procedure for documenting the major actions required, when, and by whom, during the phases of development, manufacture, distribution, and operational use of the system. This documentation insures that all the participatory organizations, both those under the authority chain of the system manager and those associated by contractual arrangement, or mutual interest—such as dealers or distributing organizations, and customers or user organizations—are aware of the objectives of the system and the major decisions to be made in the system life. Necessary funding is a major requirement, and so is resource allocation. Major control points or milestones are usually developed with provisions for detailed progress reviews at each milestone.

Changes of an anticipated or unanticipated nature occur with startling regularity. To cope with them, advance provisions must be made. Some changes may be due to technological progress, but other changes may be brought about by economic, social, and political factors. To understand the cost of the system, all costs—the training of personnel to develop, manufacture, test, distribute, use, maintain, and perhaps recyle the system —are developed. Costs of test equipment, the development of test procedures, the construction of necessary facilities for research, manufacture, testing, and storage, and the training of user or customer personnel should also be included. An estimate of the life span of the operational phase is made to provide for the identification of a replacement, or follow-on, or next-generation system. This documentation can be developed by cluster of interest—e.g., development cost, manpower cost, distribution cost, storage cost, manufacturing cost, procurement cost—or by area of responsibility—system manager responsibility, user or customer responsibility, training responsibility, responsibility by contractual arrangement. Detailed plans and documentation are developed for all procurement, including raw materials, purchased parts, computer time sharing, and test facilities. Manpower build-up, availability of facilities, and schedules of all supporting subsystems are needed by all participants.

If the life of the system is to be in the phases described, dependent upon review of results and approval of go-ahead advancement to the next phase, the membership and qualifications of all members of each review committee or board, which are highly important, should be specified. The possiblity of contingency approvals—i.e., approvals given with the understanding that certain specified actions will be taken—should be addressed and clarifying procedures developed. Responsibility for approval of corrective action and the removal of the contingency circumstances should be specified by documentation, and courses of action recommended to remove all contingencies by a specified date.

Configuration base lines must be developed and formal procedures established for maintaining control of changes in configuration. (Configuration management documentation is discussed in the next chapter.) The costs of configuration management procedures—even though a very small fraction of total system costs—must be identified and included in the total system cost.

Documentation describing the logistics needs to be developed to make provision for maintainability and reliability, maintenance, support equipment, test equipment, supply support, transportability, transportation, packaging and handling, and technical data; i.e., instructions for use. All system documentation is transferred to the logistic-support manager at the time he assumes responsibility for management of the system.

ORGANIZATION OF THE SYSTEM MANAGEMENT OFFICE

Since a system includes not only hardware but related facilities, equipment, material services, and the personnel required for its operation, the staff of the system management office would logically be composed of qualified representatives—whether individual persons or groups—representing each of the pertinent areas. Actually, the organization of the system management office is far more a reflection of the outlook, ability, and desires of the system manager; the various operative areas, however, are usually represented, and the following discussion is based on that premise.

The system management office deserves a capability in the areas of procurement, production, engineering, configuration management, financial management, training, logistics, testing, program control, user or customer liaison, plans or documentation, and integration. The system manager will, of course, develop the type of organization which he or she believes to be most effective under the given set of circumstances. Experience has shown, however, that the inclusion of specialists from all the areas enumerated, accountable to the system manager by authority/responsibility lines of communication and control, will prove a valuable asset. The system manager needs help to discharge his or her responsibilities by assuming accountability for all the decisions made in the business, engineering, and contractual areas, for interfaces with other participants, and for all system changes, both technical and administrative. A brief look at the recommended staff may help further to indicate the magnitude and complexities of the system manager's responsibilities.

PROGRAM CONTROL

The function of the program control office is very important. The system manager relies on this staff to maintain current records, which provide him or her with the capability to ascertain the system status of any given area instantaneously. Another important task is to state clearly the system's financial objectives and plans. To accomplish this requires the preparation of budgets, the allocation of financial resources, and the preparation of costs and schedule changes associated with both engineering and administration. If the organization employs PERT, program control specialists prepare and maintain a status chart on the overall system and prepare subsystem status reports. But, whether or not PERT is used, a control room, with charts showing the current status of problem areas, is an invaluable tool for the system manager. Such a room is used to obtain a quick, highly visible report of the current status of problem areas and to determine which needs immediate personal attention. The control room is an option, of course, but it represents an excellent way of keeping track of the current status of each subsystem, and of having each system's plan and budget and cost record open, readily available for review, and displayed in such a fashion that only the exceptions require attention. The use of the control room and display procedures vary from organization to organization, but they should always be tailored to meet a given system's needs and the system manager's wishes.

ENGINEERING

The members of the engineering staff located in the system management office are usually accountable in every respect—for tenure, for promotion, for termination of employment, for salary increases, as well as for performance evaluation—to the system manager. They therefore serve as an interface with the other engineers in the organization—perhaps a larger group located in an engineering department. They also are in close contact with contractors and subcontractors and with whatever engineering consultants are utilized. (Some organizations use consulting engineers in both supervisory and working capacities.)

The tasks of the engineering staff include system analysis, the design of the system and its subsystems, of testing and check-out equipment, and of any unusual technological equipment needed. Some system managers place members of the engineering staff in the plants of contractors and subcontractors—with the contractors' approval, of course, and with contractual coverage. This "co-location" plan seems to help in the technical integration and assurance of technical compatibility in all system elements. Still another major task of the engineering staff is the development of system specifications, engineering drawings, and the initiation or review of all changes in those specifications and drawings.

PROCUREMENT AND PRODUCTION

Frequently the responsibilities and activities concerned with procurement and production are combined in the system management office. It is this staff that is responsible for the initiation, negotiation, and completion of all contracting and procurement actions and alterations, including the commitment of funds and the supervision of quality-assurance activities by contractors and subcontractors. In the contractual area, it is responsible for the type of contract selected—the performance guarantees, the incentive provisions, the contract options to be utilized, and the definition of the responsibility for total system performance; it also handles all arrangements about the correction of deficiencies, the liquidation of damages, and any and all other necessary contractual arrangements. This group usually serves as cost analysts in price redetermination or in any similar changes.

It is this staff of experts that reviews production management and production engineering activities, oversees whatever physical facilities are required to insure they are adequate for production of the system, insures the delivery to the contractor of any parts or equipment or facilities promised, and makes recommendations about such decisions as to whether to manufacture or buy certain parts.

CONFIGURATION MANAGEMENT

The "configuration" of an item or system describes its function and physical characteristics. The maintenance of the current description of a system and all its designated items is a task of tremendous magnitude. (A detailed discussion of the configuration management staff function is the subject of the next chapter. Here we will only briefly review some of the functions of this very important area.) Configuration management, as we have already noted, deserves—and is receiving—increasing attention by system manufacturers.

The configuration management staff is responsible for formalizing all the system requirements into an overall system specification, in order to control the hardware configuration, and to account for every configuration or end item in the system. An early task is to select which items are to be controlled. Once an item has been designated as a configuration or end item, any proposed change in such an item must be formally considered and approved. This applies, of course, to proposals for change, approved by the engineering staff—they are likewise controlled by the configuration management staff. Data management—the acquisition of data about changes— is another function of this group. This staff of experts establishes procedures to be followed prior to the development and acceptance of a configuration base line for the system—a major milestone in the life of the system. The group also develops procedures for handling proposals for configuration change—often through the establishment of a board or committee to consider the proposed changes and their acceptance, modification, or rejection.

These specialists closely follow the initiation and control of a program to insure the timely completion of system specifications. They may develop a configuration status accounting system with periodic reports to keep the system manager fully aware of the system status. Such a reporting system is very important to the system manager and may well be presented in a control room. These specialists normally assume the task of data management for the system. The objective of configuration management, then, is not necessarily to prevent changes in the system but to provide a mechanism for accommodating any changes made and properly to document and account for them and the adjustments made in the equipment. When the owner of some make of automobile is notified to return his or her car to the dealer for adjustments in some part found defective, this notification is made possible by one facet of configuration management.

TEST AND DEPLOYMENT

The test and deployment experts in the system management office prepare plans for overall system test and deployment. This includes the programming for test facilities and instrumentation, planning for bench testing, static testing, subsystems testing, and finally for integrated system testing. It is the test and deployment staff that determine the acceptability of test results, the number of systems and subsystems required for test programs, the adequacy of test instrumentation to insure achievement of test objectives; it is also their responsibility to insure the training of whatever personnel are required for the various test programs. Deployment or distribution plans, including any warehousing or storage plans, and the time phasing of distribution are also responsibilities normally discharged by this group.

LOGISTIC SUPPORT

The logistic support personnel in the system management office are, as are all other specialist personnel, accountable to the system manager. As we have mentioned previously, in the case of major systems, it is reasonable to expect that the senior specialist will become the system manager in the operational or deployment phase of the system life cycle. Such a transfer of responsibility may or may not entail a geographic transfer of personnel. The logistic support staff provides advice and recommendations concerning logistic support during the planning and development phase of the system. It advises on the source selection of contractors and subcontractors, and plays an important part in planning and assuring logistic support during system testing. It insures that logistic supportability is considered in all decisions, determines what numbers of what types of spare parts are ordered or provisioned for users, and plans for and implements the modification of delivered equipment. A very important function of this group is the provision of engineering support to the system during the operational or logistic management phase of the system life cycle. In addition, the logistic support specialists provide figures on provisioning costs and spare-parts costs to the system manager for budget purposes.

In summary, we see that the system manager is responsible for the system, that program control plans for the system, that the engineering specialists determine what the system is, that the test and deployment specialists test the system, that the configuration management specialists control the system, that the procurement and production specialists buy the system, and that the logistic support specialists support the system.

In considering the responsibilities of the system manager, it is interesting to note how his or her authority in the development and acquisition of major military systems has been expanded or strengthened through the years. Some fifteen years ago the manager of a military system perceived the inadequacy of the system manager's authority. He queried, formally, other military system managers about their perceptions concerning the amount of authority delegated to them. Fifty-four percent of the system managers responding, or nineteen out of the thirty-five participating, reported the use of a committee or board meeting as a substitute for authority, and 61 percent, or twenty out of thirty-three, believed that more authority delegated to the system manager would reduce acquisition costs. Less than half of those system managers queried, or fourteen out of thirty-two, were of the opinion that they had sufficient authority (Lanford).

Current acquisition policies of the military departments are much less structured now than they were earlier. More authority has been delegated to the system manager, and this authority is stressed to a greater degree than before. Present policies allow a large degree of flexibility to the system manager.[1] The authority delegated to the civilian-sector system

---

1.   The reader is invited to compare the current Air Force Regulations 800 series, governing acquisition management and implementing Department of Defense Directive 5000.1, Acquisition of Major Defense Systems, with the earlier Air Force Regulations 375 series for system management.

manager is easier to determine and measure. Suffice it to say, that the system manager, whether military or civilian, must possess sufficient authority to enable him or her to manage a very complex, many-faceted system. This authority must be delegated and cannot be dependent upon the ability of the system manager to build alliances as a substitute for authority. He or she does not have the time.

6... CONFIGURATION MANAGEMENT

INTRODUCTION

So far, the reader has had an opportunity to consider a philosophy of management, the bureaucratic form of organization, conflict in system management, and the system management office. This chapter discusses configuration management, already an important part of system management, with the expectation that it will become of even greater importance in the near future.[1] The importance of configuration management was first brought forcefully to the attention of industry and the military in the 1950s at the time of the development of early ground-launched missiles.

In a symposium on configuration management held on the West Coast, an executive of a major airframe manufacturer stated that his company, as well as every other aerospace company, was in business for one reason only—to make a profit. Profit, he added, comes through effective cost control, and effective cost control comes through the proper identification of each task to be performed. This executive further pointed out that through such identification one can effectively estimate, negotiate, and control costs and that the proper identification of these

---

1. AFSCM/AFLCM 375-7, *Configuration Management for Systems, Equipment, Munitions, and Computer Programs,* Department of the Air Force, Headquarters Air Force Systems Command, 31 March 1971, is the basis for the development of this chapter. Attention is also invited to Military Standard MIL-STD-480, *Configuration Control, Engineering Changes, Deviations and Waivers,* 30 October 1968, and to *Systems Management,* Aeronautical Systems Division Manual ASDM 375-3, Headquarters, Aeronautical Systems Division, Air Force Systems Command, 15 February 1963.

activities provides a base line, which is a key word in configuration management. It is through the establishment of a configuration base line, and through effective management, that an organization has the opportunity to achieve a profit (McCarthy).

CONFIGURATION MANAGEMENT DEFINED

The term "configuration" refers to the functional and physical characteristics of a hardware or software product. The technical parameters of the system, its equipment and subsystems must be completely documented, and the end product must conform to this technical description. As the anecdote about the missile makes apparent, a manufacturer must be able to duplicate his or her original product. Configuration management is a set of procedures by which a system and its components are accurately described; a detailed record of all changes in the system or components maintained, including the technical achievements of the change, status reports on the progress of the change, the systems affected by the change, and where the systems of each particular configuration are located. The purpose of configuration management is to assure that with each physical or functional change, the necessary alterations are also made in technical documentation, in the description, in test and check-out maintenance, in spare-parts and supply procedures. Training of personnel in operation or repair may also be affected. Configuration management therefore identifies and documents the functional and physical characteristics of any item designated as a configuration item, any subsequent changes made in those characteristics, and records and reports on the status of incorporation of those changes.

To facilitate configuration management, three base lines are developed. The first is the functional base line, which describes performance (speed, range, safety), operating parameters, and logistic requirements. The second is the allocated base line; the third is the product base line. Postponing until later a discussion of why an item is designated a configuration item, let us assume that a major item—a jet engine, for example—has been designated a configuration item. A functional base line, describing power output, allowable temperatures, fuel consumption, reliability requirements, maintainability requirements, and perhaps, safety requirements, will be developed for the engine itself, and an allocated base line for the engine's major components. The major components—the burner, the compressor, the first-stage turbine, the second-stage turbine, and the control system—will then each have an allocated base line. The performance expected of the engine will result in documenting the demands or the functional characteristics that are required of each of the major components. In other words, the allocated base line contains the specifications of each particular component. The allocated base line also includes a description of the tests necessary to achieve the allocated functional requirements, any design constraints on the component, and requirements or specifications concerning interfaces with the other configuration items.

The third or product base line describes the product configuration—all the physical and functional characteristics of the item from the time of its delivery from the factory door through customer use, maintenance and repair, and logistic support. This base line also documents a description of all tests necessary to prove that the final item meets its specified requirements. At the risk of oversimplification, the product base line also changes with a series (or model) change incorporating changes or improvements in the product, as will the other base lines.

FIG. 6.1: THE CONFIGURATION MANAGEMENT TASK

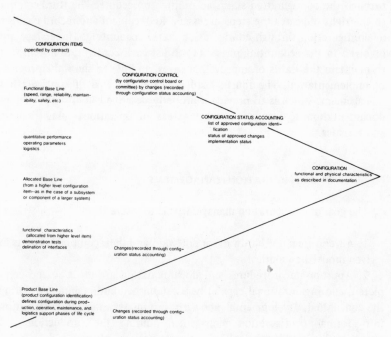

Figure 6.1 conceptualizes the task of configuration management and what that task requires. The left-hand column shows the steps necessary to identify and document the functional and physical characteristics of any configuration item—the first step in configuration management. Note

the development of the three base lines necessary: the functional base line, the allocated base line, and the product base line. Figure 6.1 shows the functional base line describing such characteristics as speed, range, reliability, maintainability, and safety. The development of the functional base line includes consideration of quantitative performance, operating parameters, and logistic requirements. The allocated base line, which contains the specifications for all the components or subsystems, includes consideration of functional characteristics, demonstration tests to show achievement of the functional objectives, and the delineation of interfaces. The product base line is the approved configuration of the product which will exist during the production and use of the end item or system.

The second column to the right in Figure 6.1 indicates the method of documenting changes in the functional and physical characteristics of a configuration item—the second stage in configuration management. Any and all changes in any of the base lines are accomplished through a committee or configuration control board, and these changes are then recorded through the configuration status accounting procedure. The third column to the right indicates the steps necessary to document and record changes in configuration through configuration status accounting. Three steps are involved in the accounting phase: (1) to list each configuration item, (2) to maintain the status of approved changes, and (3) to show the progress of implementation. The fourth head indicates the goal of configuration management, which is to provide a properly described item supported by documentation to insure support in areas of operational use, training, and logistics.

PURPOSE OF CONFIGURATION MANAGEMENT

The goal of configuration management is to insure that

1. All end items of hardware or software and their component parts in a given model are identical.

2. Appropriate procedures and documentation are initiated and completed, and organizational capability is established and maintained during the conceptual, developmental, and early-test phases to facilitate transition into formal configuration management during the production and operational-in-service—or deployment customer-use—phases.

3. Delivered end items of equipment and subsystems are accurately and completely described in all identifying documentation.

4. For every approved change in the functional or physical characters of an end item, corresponding changes are made to the extent applicable

in all related support elements. (Such support elements are the special equipment needed to maintain and operate the system, e.g., the ground equipment necessary to support an aircraft system—such as starters, passenger-loading passageways, tow tractors—special tooling needed for depot overhaul and repair, spare parts, training equipment, technical instructions for operation or repair, engineering data, check-out operational and maintenance computer programs, and associated records.)

5. There exists a configuration record for each end item documenting every approved change.

6. Every change involving more than one configuration control committee or board will be fully coordinated prior to implementation.

7. The specific location and status of every end item of equipment or subsystems that have been selected as configuration items are known by part number and serial number at all times during the production and operational phases.

8. Every proposal for change in system equipment, subsystem, or facility is evaluated and resolved by a qualified configuration control committee or board.

9. Management achieves with the lowest costs that are sound, the required performance, operational efficiency, logistic support, and readiness in all configuration items.

10. The maximum degree of latitude in design and development is allowed. Care must, however, be taken to insure the degree and depth of configuration control necessary for production and logistic support.

11. Maximum efficiency in the management of configuration changes is obtained with respect to their necessity, cost, timing, and implementation.

SELECTION OF ITEMS

The final selection of which items are subject to configuration procedures is a personal decision of the system manager; it is also a slowly evolving process. The choice is determined by the system manager's need to control a given item's characteristics or to control the interface of that item with other items. This selection is outwardly accomplished through the system engineering process, which is based on such factors as the requirement that (1) all units are designed to one configuration-item specification; (2) all units of hardware be identified by a top assembly drawing; (3) all computer programs be identified by one top flow chart accompanied by subordinate flow charts; and (4) the end use of the identification is designed to serve as the foundation for providing spare parts or for the preparation of operating and maintenance manuals.

No set of rules can ever obviate the factor of individual personal judgment in deciding which items should be designated configuration items. Here, however, are some considerations or suggestions that may be helpful to the system manager:

1. The product base line is established on hardware items at the factory door upon delivery of the first article. The configuration of this first article must therefore be known, so that any later changes to delivered systems can start from this established reference point.

2. Sufficient information must be available for the item to be designated.

3. The item selected must be at a level that permits release of engineering changes at a top assembly level.

4. When an item that will provide a separate or additional capability is considered as an add-on assembly, the designation of the add-on assembly as a configuration item may assist in scheduling activities.

5. A configuration item should have a common installation and deployment requirement; in other words, if a system has both ground and airborne subsystems, two configuration item designations should be made—one for the ground and the other for the airborne package.

6. Perhaps the best guideline is the realization that the selection of configuration items requires analysis of both the technical and the administrative implications. There is no stylized workable description of a configuration item other than it is to be an end product that has been formally accepted as such by the system management office.

7. Computer programs are, however, classified separately—not as part of a hardware item. Separate capabilities or capabilities delivered at different times may be designated as individual configuration items. In general, operation, utility, and diagnostic programs should be individual configuration items. Computer programs with potential use in multiple systems should be separate configuration items, whereas highly interrelated computer programs are best combined in one configuration.

8. In determining the selection of items for documentation, it is well worthwhile to remember that to set the level too high, resulting in too few configuration items, is less than practical from an engineering design and manufacturing standpoint in addressing and controlling change. On the other hand, if the level is too low, resulting in too many configuration items, the administrative tasks become burdensome and costly. Expertise in selecting configuration items—large or small, complex or simple—comes with experience.

9. During the development and initial production phases, every item that is directly referred to in a contract is automatically designated as a

configuration item. During the operation and maintenance phases, any repairable component that is available for separate procurement is so designated. Once such a component has been selected as a configuration item, technical documentation (configuration identification) describing the part in specifications and drawing is prepared.

Many system managers find the preparation of a system allocation document—identifying the whole aggregation of configuration items that make up the system—useful to show the location of designated items by serial number.

The fact that the identification of configuration items is a slowly evolving process has already been mentioned. The degree of completeness of the documentation is governed by what phase in the life cycle the system is in, as well as by its purpose or objective.

PHASES OF CONFIGURATION MANAGEMENT

This section describes the configuration management activities that take place during the five phases of the life cycle of a system.

FIG. 6.2: A CONFIGURATION MANAGEMENT VIEW OF THE SYSTEM LIFE CYCLE

CONCEPTUAL PHASE		VALIDATION PHASE		DESIGN & DEVELOPMENT PHASE		PRODUCTION PHASE	OPERATIONAL PHASE
	Functional Base Line		Allocated Base Line		Product Base Line	Beginning of the Preparation of Status Accounting Reports	
determination of technical feasibility, cost effectiveness studies, and determination of preferred approach		functional configuration identification		allocation configuration identification		product configuration identification	In-Service Status Accounting Reports

Figure 6.2 shows these five phases of the system from the configuration management point of view. Note that the functional base line is developed as a result of the conceptual phase; the allocated base line, or functional configuration identification, as a result of the validation phase; the product base line, or allocation configuration identification, as a result of the design and development phase; and that status-accounting reports begin with the product base line at the beginning of the production phase and continue through the operational phase.

The configuration item specifications are used as contractual instruments to control the design and development of each configuration item during the production phase. Attention should be given to the preparation of whatever interface control documentation is necessary during the validation phase. Any additional configuration items not previously identified can be documented as design and development progresses.

The configuration management office must review each configuration item specification and establish the configuration base lines. As we have already stated, the conceptual phase should result in the establishment of the functional base line; the validation phase in the establishment of the allocated base line; the design and development phase, in the establishment of the product base line. With the entry into the production phase, the initiation of status-accounting reports occurs.

CONCEPTUAL PHASE

During the conceptual phase, the effort is primarily oriented toward the establishment of definitive requirements for the new system under consideration. Firm and realistic specifications are established; interfaces are defined; the responsibility for the management of each interface determined; high risk areas of technology are highlighted, and the "best," or at least an acceptable, technical approach selected. The functional base line is developed as a result of the conceptual phase.

VALIDATION PHASE

The validation phase is the formulative stage in the evolution of a system during which the major trade-offs are accomplished. During this phase, the need for a given capability is defined in the system specifications which establish quality requirements as well as technical requirements and are then translated and allocated into performance requirements for individual configuration items. During this period the emphasis is on system engineering, system analysis, and prototyping. Technical management and configuration management are accomplished at the system level. Formal configuration management to establish the functional base line should, however, be implemented early in the validation phase—at the point the system specifications are approved.

The system manager needs to know as early in the life cycle as possible whether the demands of the specifications are being met in a realistic way. The validation phase serves as an opportunity to verify or prove out the technical characteristics that describe the system and to which the system must conform. This is accomplished first through analysis and then through hardware development.

Many system managers find it useful to develop a work-breakdown chart or product-oriented family tree (see Fig. 6.3). Conceptually, unlike most family trees, this one is concerned with the inverted tree or root structure. Beginning at "ground level," if you will, there is both vertical and lateral development of the root structure. It begins at ground level— or the top level—with the major system or end product and develops both vertically and laterally into major components, subassemblies, component parts, and bits and pieces—the lowest level or discrete parts— visualized as the tiny outgrowths at the extremities of the root system. Such a work-breakdown chart, which can show both hardware and software if called for, thus identifies every task required for the design, fabrication, assembly, and testing of the system. With it the system manager can see the relation of one component to another. It can also be invaluable if used as an overlay on a functional organization chart and thus be used to determine what organizational group is responsible for accomplishing each work task. Those places where the work-breakdown structure, or family tree intersects with the functional organization chart represent tasks and are known as workboxes. These workboxes serve many purposes: (1) to estimate the time and cost, including material, of accomplishing a given task; (2) to show who is to accomplish each task; (3) to show what subassembly a part serves; (4) to record the amount of actual cost required to perform as opposed to the estimated cost; and (5) to keep track of accountability.

FIG. 6.3:   LEVELS OF DEVELOPMENT

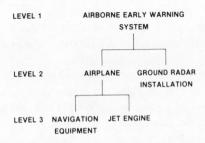

Adding up the actual cost to accomplish each workbox of each part, subassembly, assembly, and major component and comparing it with the estimated cost of the total system allows the system manager to determine whether the system is in an overrun position and, if so, to learn where the problem is. From this information, the manager can determine the cost and performance efficiencies experienced to date, determine the time and cost until completion, and thus the work performance needed to complete the system within budgeted costs.

To return to the development of the work-breakdown structure, the identification of three levels, at least, has been found necessary. Level one is the entire system; level two includes the major elements of the system, for example, an airplane, a radar installation, or aggregations of services, data, and activities, such as system test and evaluation. Level three includes the components subordinate to level two but nevertheless such major elements as, for example, a jet engine, an electric plant, or a type of service, such as a technical evaluation.

The system manager will want to fill the position of configuration manager early in the validation phase. The configuration manager must then determine the manpower requirements immediately needed for his or her configuration management group, must look ahead toward the need for additional personnel, and must plan for the implementation of the system configuration management procedures. His or her primary mission during the validation phase will be to make certain that all system participants understand configuration management requirements. A major task facing the configuration manager is to explain and implement configuration identification functions and plan the preparation of accurate specifications and related engineering data.

Configuration management activities, as we have already emphasized, are of great importance during the validation phase. The system manager will find he or she needs to appoint to the configuration control committee or board a member from each participating organization—who, incidentally, should have signatory power to act as its representative—to manage changes in the initial system specifications. The configuration management plan may be made a contractual requirement if the entire system is to be acquired from a contractor. If this is the case, the contractor will need to develop an internal group and procedures to accomplish configuration management requirements.

The development of the system specifications, with all its ramifications, should be completed in the validation phase. The specifications will describe the functional base line of the system and the allocated base lines of all components. As mentioned earlier, an important task to be accomplished in the validation phase is the preparation of plans for interface control.

DESIGN AND DEVELOPMENT PHASE

This phase includes the design and full-scale development of the entire system and of each configuration item. Realistic cost estimates and delivery schedules are developed in this phase. All configuration items are integrated into the system and the product base line is developed. The configuration manager may then implement status-accounting reports upon the completion of the product base line.

The three base lines designed to facilitate configuration management—the functional base line, the allocated base line, and the product base line—have at this point been developed. After the product base line has been developed, management of configuration items is accomplished at the individual item level. To assist in the control of individual items, a configuration item development specification is usually prepared, giving the performance and qualifications expected of each individual item. This document should also describe interface requirements with other items or with other organizations.

The idea of building to or contracting to given base lines is not new. In fact, a contract has always been a base line from which to proceed, according to Herbert C. Courington, an aerospace-industry executive. He has said that whether the business is aerospace, electronics, construction, advertising, or insurance, whenever a customer and a contractor make an agreement for the future delivery of a product or service, that agreement—or contract—defines what is expected, but that since both contractor and customer are human, changes will surely be made. The fact that changes are to be expected serves to point up the importance of the original contract as the base line to be followed.

Base-line contracting, Courington observes, has a number of advantages for both the contractor and the customer. Advantages for the contractor include (1) protection from varying interpretations of requirements by replacement personnel—the better the definition, the more precise the specification, the less the chance for interpretation; (2) the contractor is better able to hold the customer to contract specifications—i.e., no "extras"—for each requirement is clearly defined; (3) there should be no schedule slippage because of funding problems; (4) once there is an adequate base line, later changes can more easily be negotiated. The advantages for the customer are (1) the customer gets what he or she bargained for—which is presumably what he or she wants; (2) because of fewer changes, owing to better specifications, the costs will almost surely be lower; (3) well-defined base lines are an aid in any modification of plans and programs; (4) the contractor and the customer know exactly what is wanted—resulting in better contractor performance; and (5) the contracting agency can show auditors or senior management how well the system is being managed toward achievement of objectives.

CONFIGURATION AUDITS

The configuration audit is a means of verifying whether configuration items match specifications and authorized changes. The function of the audit is to insure the accomplishment of development requirements and the achievement of a production configuration through a comparison of a prototype or first-production item with its technical description. There are two kinds of audits that may be performed—the functional and the physical.

A functional audit reviews an end item's test or analysis data to verify that the item performs as intended. A physical audit involves the matching of an "as-built" item with its technical documentation to insure that the documentation is complete and establishes the product base line, is suitable for use in follow-on production, is satisfactory to use in accepting items, and is acceptable for operational, maintenance, and logistic support purposes.

QUALIFICATION OF CONFIGURATION ITEMS

In order to confirm that configuration items do, in fact, meet specifications and performance requirements, the system manager also conducts tests, inspections, and utilizes analytical processes to qualify the items—that is, assures that the item meets its specifications. The qualification record is maintained as part of the configuration management files.

PRODUCTION PHASE

The production phase begins with the contractual "go ahead" for production of the system and ends with the delivery of the final system to the customer.[2] Most system managers find it necessary to implement a

---

2.   Some writers refer to the "acquisition phase." The acquisition phase would presumably encompass the activities of both the full-scale development phase and the production phase.

configuration status accounting system during the production phase. Configuration status accounting is the recording and reporting of the information needed to manage product documentation effectively. This product documentation information includes a listing of the approved configuration identification, the status of proposed changes to configuration, and the implementation status of all approved changes. Generally, status accounting reports are begun once the product base line has been determined, but never later than at the beginning of the production phase. They continue through the operational phase, but the responsibility for them is transferred to the logistics management office at the end of the production phase.

Joseph F. Dietle, an executive responsible for the configuration accounting function in an aerospace firm, finds necessary both the configuration identification index, which indicates the ultimate design objectives of system hardware, and a configuration status accounting report that indicates the scheduling and completion of all actions and events required to accomplish the incorporation of the ultimate design objective in the hardware. Through the accurate, complete, and timely maintenance of a configuration status accounting report, the configuration manager can keep his or her finger on the pulse of the entire operation of incorporating engineering changes into the program. Furthermore, Dietle says, the manager can thus become aware of those potential downstream problems that exist because scheduled actions and events have not been accomplished. The configuration status accounting report points up these slippages and potential problems.

A configuration identification index is an indispensable part of the configuration management scheme. It is a listing of all the configuration items in the system at a given time, and it is published every thirty days. The configuration identification index and the status accounting report should be tailored to each particular system so that only the information really necessary to manage configuration effectively and economically appears. (My own experience with a number of systems has shown that the cost of configuration management is only a small fraction of the system contract cost, varying from 1/8 of 1 percent to 1/30 of 1 percent in the eight major systems examined.) The identification index identifies an item's approved identification, and the status accounting report continuously tracks changes in the approved configuration, along with priorities, schedules, and progress of change implementation. The recording of this information is of great assistance in troubleshooting.

The configuration manager is usually faced with a decision of whether it is more economical to prepare these reports manually or through the use of an automated data-processing machine. Experience favors manual reporting, unless the great volume of data to be handled makes automatic data processing more economical. Consultation with experienced data-automation management personnel can be most helpful in making this determination.

The system manager should assist the configuration manager in applying common sense in the use of control devices. Overselection of configuration items or duplication of control may result in voluminous reports and inaccuracies in data that will cause a decrease of confidence in the configuration system. Adequate control, as we have seen, begins with the selection of only those items that can be managed, continues with proper planning and understanding, and culminates in the wise use of control reports.

OPERATIONAL PHASE

The operational phase for a configuration item begins with the delivery of the first item to the customer. The transition of configuration management from the system management office to the support or logistics manager is usually made early in the operational phase. The transfer of management responsibility includes the physical transfer of all records, including the complete file of specifications and changes, the complete file of configuration-item data, and is normally preceded by an agreement as to the future chairing of the configuration-control committee. The logistics manager processes all proposed engineering changes, modification programs, or "quick-fix" programs as may be necessary during the operational life of the system—and some systems, as we have already seen, have very long operational lives.

We have now traced the development of some of the elements in configuration management: first, the identification of configuration items; second, the listing of all configuration items in a configuration identification index; and third, the status-accounting report. Status accounting—the bookkeeping part of configuration management—provides the configuration manager, other functional managers, and the system manager with feedback information to determine whether the decisions of the configuration control committee are being implemented. It also provides managers with the visibility to permit follow-through on directives and helps to insure that schedules are maintained by the members of participating organizations and individuals.

We have emphasized the necessity for a configuration—or change—control committee, and noted that it is wise for representatives from all participating organizations to be members of it. Change control, which is the fourth element, is the most visible aspect of configuration management. As we have seen, the change-control committee evaluates and approves or disapproves all proposals for engineering change and requests for deviations and waivers of technical requirements.

The purpose of change control is to prevent unneeded or marginal changes, yet at the same time to expedite the approval and implementation of desirable ones—those that are necessary or that promise significant benefit to the operational cost or support capabilities of the system. Examples of desirable changes are those that correct deficiencies, significantly improve operational effectiveness or reduce logistic support requirements, that offer substantial life-cycle cost savings, and that prevent slippage in production schedules. Change control also includes the functions of setting change priorities—which may be immediately compelling, which urgent, and which routine—and of assuring that necessary instructions and funding authorizations are issued promptly for approved changes. Once the technical requirements—that is, the functional base line, the allocated base line, and the product base line of the system and its configuration items—have been documented, each decision to change the technical requirements and the associated documentation should be formally approved by the chairman of the configuration control committee or board.

The configuration control committee seems to function best when it is an appendage of the system management office. In addition to the chairman and regular members, alternate members are usually designated. The configuration control committee serves in an advisory capacity to the chairman—it is not a voting committee. It is expected to develop policies regarding changes, but the committee chairman is accountable for all final decisions regarding changes. Members disagreeing with the chairman's decision are free to document their dissenting opinions. The dissenting opinion should be developed in detail and may well be made a part of the committee-proceedings file.

The system manager is usually the chairman of the change committee, although he may select an alternate chairman. The configuration manager will want to be the committee's secretary. All functional managers of the system management office and other participating organizations are expected to provide representatives as committee members.

To plan for his or her control functions, the configuration manager, during the full-scale development phase, establishes an environmental and administrative framework to (1) facilitate base-line specification reviews; (2) control changes to the base lines; and (3) facilitate development of product specifications for configuration items. As the production phase arrives and continues, the control function increases in emphasis, and the configuration control committee develops close coordination with the many interested activities. It goes without saying that once the product base line has been established, the status accounting function becomes as demanding as the functions of identification and control.

7 ... FUTURE ENVIRONMENTAL FACTORS

The aim of this chapter is to impress upon the system manager the importance of the surrounding social and cultural environment and draw attention to the numerous factors that contribute to it.

The system manager of the present, as well as of the future, must be ever aware of changes and trends that contribute to the social, political, economic, and general technological scene. These four areas by no means represent the entire environment, but they exemplify the factors about which the successful system manager should be cognizant (other areas include the psychological, the religious, and numerous others).

A look at the expected or likely future can be accomplished through using a scenario—a projection into the future of present conditions modified by foreseen or expected changes and assumptions. A relatively simple scenario will be sketched in each of the several areas and integrated into a picture of the expected future. Science-fiction novels and stories have much in common with such a scenario. The writer of science fiction envisions the future for his or her own purposes, and a number of science-fiction authors in the past have proved to be uncannily accurate in their forecasts. For instance, "Buck Rogers"—a comic strip of the 1930s—portrayed space travel, rocket propulsion, rocket belts for human beings, ray guns, and other devices that have since come to pass.

THE SOCIAL SCENARIO

Any social scenario of the future is difficult to develop because social trends are slow to evince themselves and because sufficient time must elapse in order to distinguish a trend from a "fad."[1] At present, a growing number of social scientists are interested in developing the capability of the scenario to project the future, and indications are that increasing emphasis will be placed on this device.

Herman Kahn and Barry Bruce-Briggs, two experienced observers, divide the development of society into four major stages: (1) the pre-agricultural stage, lasting until about 8000 B.C.; (2) the agricultural society, lasting until about A.D. 1800; (3) the industrial stage, brought about by the industrial revolution, lasting until the third quarter of the twentieth century; and (4) modern society, which they view as now entering the latest stage—postindustrial society—signs of which are already apparent and which will certainly be here by the year 2000.

Herman Kahn cites five characteristics which he attributes to post-industrial society (1974): (1) the change from a goods-producing to a service society, (2) the preeminence of the professional and technical class, (3) the predominance of theoretical knowledge as the source of innovation and policy formulation, (4) the creation of new intellectual technology, and (5) the possibility of self-sustaining technological growth.

Defining postindustrial society as one in which the service sector accounts for more than half of the total employment and more than half of the Gross National Product, Kahn reports that the United States is the first country to have entered this stage. He finds a major change occurring in our society in the growth of professional and technical employment—for which there is the requirement of some college education. He cites the fact that in 1964 there were 8.6 million persons in this category, and the number has been projected to reach 15.5 million by the end of 1980. Within this group, there has been an extraordinary rise in the number of scientists and engineers, who will hold the key to postindustrial society. While the growth rate of the professional and technical class has been double that of the labor force as a whole, the growth rate of scientists and engineers has been triple that of the working population as a whole.

---

1. The social scenario is based on a paper, "The Social Scenario," presented by Richard J. Moff, National Cash Register Corporation, at a Technological Forecasting Conference, American Management Associations Center, Chicago, Illinois, December 3, 1974. The scenario has been updated as necessary.

In postindustrial society, theoretical rather than empirical knowledge will take precedence in making decisions and maintaining control of change. According to Kahn, increasing amounts of theoretical knowledge will be codified into abstract systems of symbols and employed in decision making. He forecasts that what small advances are made in economics, science, and technology will depend primarily on the codification of theoretical knowledge and that there will therefore be an increasing dependence on universities, research laboratories, and institutes where such codification takes place.

Intellectual technology, according to Kahn, refers to the various techniques of linear programming, system analysis, information theory, decision theory, game theory, and simulation, which linked to a computer extend the intellectual powers of humankind. With the marriage of these techniques with computers, large aggregates of data can be accumulated and manipulated so as to create controlled experiments in the social sciences and to trace out the progressive and regressive consequences of alternative courses of action.

Kahn finds that a postindustrial society, in order to avoid stagnation, must open up new technological frontiers in order to maintain production and expansion. He foresees the development of new forecasting and mapping techniques to facilitate a new phase in economic history—the conscious planned advance of technological growth.

SOME SOCIAL TRENDS

Although the rate of growth in the population of the United States has lessened, the population itself continues to increase, and it is projected that there will be 300 million persons by the year 2000. The advocates of zero population growth, and the publicity accompanying this group's efforts, have made the general public aware of the dangers of a steadily increasing population without concurrent planning in the social, economic, political, and technological spheres. A growing number of books have served to make our society aware of the pitfalls that lie ahead if current trends in some of these areas are allowed to go unchecked (Toffler, 1970, and Meadows, 1972). A tremendous advantage in considering forecasts of the future is that if we do not like what we see predicted, we can begin to make efforts to change the conditions or factors that presently are—or will be—working to make the undesirable forecast come true. We can alter the conditions that have produced the present trend. As the population increases, the ancillary needs which must be met are improved means of communication, an increase in geographical mobility, and as a result of our move into a postindustrial society, where there will be an increase in leisure time, a need for more recreational facilities. The housewife also will want her share of leisure time and will use ever-increasing amounts of synthetic foods, like the bacon substitute that now leads the way. Microwave ovens will be commonplace, and remote-control consoles for ordering food by home picturephone will further contribute to the leisure time available to the housewife.

Medical diagnoses through a combination of the picturephone, the computer, and specialized centers of treatment appear to be just slightly over the horizon. An increase in the use of artificial organs in human beings seems a certainty, with particular emphasis on the artificial heart. Routine treatment of physical ailments and illnesses will be increasingly in the hands of paramedics or nondegree medical assistants, who will seek the advice of fully qualified physicians only in exceptional cases. Transportation, housing, educational needs, and the like will furnish challenges not only to sociologists but also to political scientists, economists, and technologists.

Because any large system is such a long-lived item as it passes through the various phases of its life cycle, the system manager today is expected to be aware of both the present social environment and those social trends now visible which will continue to develop in the future—a period often the same as the last or operational phase of a given system. What impact—perhaps little, perhaps highly significant—can social trends have on the acceptance or utilization of the system? The supersonic transport aircraft was not acceptable to American society at the time it was proposed. Today there is frequent public clamor both for and against the location of nuclear power generating plants.

THE POLITICAL SCENARIO

The prediction of political trends remains hazardous for even the most experienced forecaster. Consolidated Analysis Centers, Incorporated (CACI), has been and is involved in analyzing data concerning political events of the past, the thought in mind being that had this information been available prior to the time of the events under study, an accurate forecast of the outcome of those events might have been made. Perhaps a model will be developed that utilizes the frequency of mention of coming political events or of political possibilities extracted from the news media. Important information to include might be the source and the perceived reliability or credibility of the source of the information. Over a period of time, the model might well develop a data base which an astute observer might use to develop a feeling of confidence—or lack thereof—in the reliability or utility of various sources.

Other technological forecasters have been active in the political area. Recognizing that a scenario may be developed in a number of ways, or by a variety of methods, one forecaster has projected the impact of some influential government agencies and the effect of such institutions on our society and thus on the system manager in the year 2000.[2]

The environment in which our political system will operate will increase in complexity and will see the political decisions of those governmental agencies controlling our society to an even greater degree. Science and technology will produce ever more complex developments; industry will grow in size, regulatory restraints will grow in power, and multinational corporations will grow in number, size, and influence. More and more members of society will pursue two careers during the course of their lives, returning to school at the end of the first career to prepare for the second one. We will continue to demand more safety in the products we buy, and we will also demand a higher degree of economic security and increased health care for ourselves and our families.

This political scenario is designed to provide food for thought, to be easily understood by the business community, and to produce expedient results, rather than to serve as a model for scholarly reflection. Each person and organization will doubtless be able to develop scenarios fitted to individual environments.

Many of our perceptions change over the course of the years; for example, at the time of the adoption of our Constitution, the four-year presidential term of office represented a far larger portion of a product's life than is the case today. It was not too many years ago that a product was conceived, a plant to produce the product constructed, operative employees trained, and the completed product was placed in the hands of consumers in a period of perhaps eighteen months. Even granted this fact the four-year presidential term of office seemed comparatively long. Today, with some products requiring a research and development period of ten years or more, with the time to build facilities and train people added on, the four-year term of office is viewed as comparatively short. Considered in this light, our political objectives certainly appear to be

---

2.   The political scenario is based on a paper, "The Political Scenario," presented by Christine Ralph MacNulty, at Technological Forecasting Conferences, American Management Associations Center, Chicago, Illinois, December 1974 and May 1975. This approach is a different but very effective technique. The scenario has been updated as necessary.

more short term than long term. It seems as if in today's environment our political system reacts to events, social, economic, scientific, and technical, rather than providing objectives and leadership.

The desire for personal and economic safety which our society manifested not long ago through its increasing interest in the subject produced a political reaction and prompted the establishment of the Department of Health, Education and Welfare. More recently, the energy crisis produced a similar reaction, resulting in the establishment of the Department of Energy. A customary governmental reaction to crisis is the establishment of a regulatory agency having an indefinite life span, which has caused the economist John Kenneth Galbraith to observe that regulatory bodies, like the bodies of those who comprise them, go through a distinct life cycle. In youth, they are vigorous, aggressive, evangelistic, and even intolerant; later they mellow; and in old age, after a matter of ten or fifteen years, they become, with some exceptions, either an arm of the industry that they are supposedly regulating or senile.

Louis M. Kohlmeier, Jr., has also observed the peculiar place that regulatory agencies occupy in our political system. He finds that they are not part of any one of the three branches of government—executive, legislative, or judicial—established in our Constitution. The agencies, he points out, are by law independent of the President's direction, yet planning is an executive function; they are virtually independent of Congress once they have been established, yet lawmaking is a legislative function; they are likewise virtually independent of the judicial branch, as evidenced by their power to pass upon obligations and privileges. Christine R. MacNulty suggests that one day we may see the regulatory agencies as a fourth branch of government, in which some of the functions of our present three branches are continued.

William L. Cary gives three requirements for a strong and viable regulatory agency: (1) a political and economic climate that will promote both public and congressional interest in the agency; (2) a program that will appeal to Congress and the public, will encourage young eager recruits, and be palatable to the industries concerned; and (3) sufficient available funds. According to this dictum, it certainly seems as if the five agencies most likely to exert the greatest amount of control over the activities of business and industry during the next twenty-five years will be the EPA (Environmental Protection Agency), the FDA (Food and Drug Administration), the EEOC (Equal Employment Opportunity Commission), the OSHA (Occupational Safety and Health Administration), and the OTAF (Office of Technology Assessment and Forecast).

EPA

The Environmental Protective Agency was created as a reaction to social concern about the problems of environmental pollution—polluted oceans, lakes, streams; air and noise pollution—which until recently neither society nor government had foreseen. It was not until after innumerable incidents of air pollution, such as at Los Angeles, Birmingham, and Donora in this country, that the government established acceptable standards for monitoring pollution. The belated campaign and efforts to restore and maintain the environment have been—and will continue to be—very costly but necessary. The effects of the energy crisis and of Three Mile Island on our environmental rehabilitation efforts is yet to be seen. A number of electric power generating plants that converted from coal to oil to nuclear fuel for power generation may be on the verge of converting back to coal. It is changes of this kind and importance that may have a significant impact upon the future of system management.

The Three Mile Island incident with its environmental implications may serve to highlight some weaknesses in the man-machine system. Some published reports have stated that monitoring devices in the Three Mile Island station showed that a problem was developing but that the warning indications were ignored—perhaps the individuals monitoring the warning devices thought, "It can't happen to this sophisticated equipment."

I am personally aware of another example in which human judgment failed to interpret signals from sophisticated equipment. An encounter between an air-launched missile and a ground-launched missile system was arranged some years ago. The element of surprise was taken away from the air-launched missile because of the necessity to suspend air traffic in the air space surrounding a city over which the air-launched missile, together with its escort aircraft—provided for safety reasons—would pass just prior to entry on to the test range. An inspection of the ground-launched missile installations showed they were located two deep astride the assumed line of flight of the air-launched missile. Inspection further showed that the most experienced personnel were assigned to the two forward installations, while less experienced personnel manned the rear installations. One of the rear installations was headed by an inexperienced manager. A decision was made to have the safety escort aircraft descend from cruise altitude in as close proximity to the air-launched missile as possible. The air-launched missile had been programmed to fly "as low as possible" over the terrain of the test site. The safety escort pilot was instructed to stay as close as possible for as long as possible to the air-launched missile in order to give a single radar target to the acquisition radar of the ground-launched missile system. The safety escort pilot was instructed to turn and fly in such a position (while flying to a safe zone) that the aircraft would present as large a target area to the radar as possible. The strategy was to force the human operators of the radar target acquisition team to make a decision when they saw a single target break into two targets—with the hope that the smaller target, the head-on view of the missile, would be temporarily ignored in the effort to track the larger target that had suddenly changed course. The strategy was successful. The missile was ignored or lost long enough for it to fly over the front installations without detection. The air-launched missile had been programmed to fly as nearly as possible over the installation headed by the new manager, the strategy being that if any ground-launched missile installation had an opportunity to fire, make it an installation manned by inexperienced people. Again, the strategy was successful. The inexperienced installation head is reported to have pressed—in the excitement of the engagement—the "no-fire" button rather than the "fire" button. No ground-launched missiles from that installation were launched. The fourth installation did launch three ground-based missiles. The air-launched missile was flying so close to the terrain that an occasional slight hill on the test range made it appear to the radar target acquisition team that the air-launched missile was flying occasionally below the surface of the ground. The three ground-based missiles launched could not be directed to a target so they flew aimlessly about like giant sky rockets.

The point being made is that regardless of the degree of sophistication of the equipment, human judgment is frequently a controlling factor. Human monitors or operators must be sufficiently trained to interpret signals received from systems. The reader is doubtless aware that any safety system devised by humans so far can also be circumvented—and frequently is—by great efforts to do so, and in some cases, with loss of human lives resulting.

Today we realize that we can no longer use the atmosphere, land, and water as dumping grounds for wastes of all kinds. Through the political process, contemporary society has shown its willingness to endure the controls that the EPA has and will establish, and also evidenced its willingness to pay for efforts to restore and conserve the environment. The costs and inconveniences of environmental restoration and conservation are already high, but aware of the unacceptable alternatives, society has no real choice. Unique conditions in certain localities—Los Angeles, for example—will require a great many more inconveniences, perhaps even real deprivation compared to the standards of convenience to which we have become accustomed, before the environment again meets acceptable standards. The system manager, as well as the consumer, is fully aware of the high but necessary costs associated with our belated efforts at environmental protection efforts. The EPA is enjoying youth in its vigorous and aggressive programs; it appears to be adequately funded. Of necessity, the controls we have known in the past but foreshadow coming controls.

FDA

The Food and Drug Administration, until relatively recently known only to the pharmaceutical and food-processing industries, seems to have received a new lease on life, thanks to the activities of consumer groups. The FDA is the agency responsible for extensive testing of drugs before they are released for sale to the public. In addition to the current demand for increased consumer protection, the realization of the disastrous side effects of certain drugs—thalidomide, for example—and the increasing use of oral contraceptives with their accompanying side effects have rekindled and revitalized the FDA. With increasing interest in health care, and the increasing use or demand for drugs of all sorts—tranquilizers, pep pills, sleeping pills, appetite inhibitors and diet foods, to mention but a few— and the research efforts this demand will stimulate in the drug industry, it is readily apparent that the controls exerted by FDA and, therefore, the influence of FDA and its effect on system managers and consumers will continue to grow.

EEOC

The Equal Employment Opportunity Commission was established as a reaction to a trend which indicated that, despite increasing levels of personal income in society as a whole, the incomes of minority groups, constituting the majority of our poor, were not keeping pace. The women's liberation movement also unquestionably has had its impact upon EEOC. In the past, there was a discernible tendency for only the outstandingly qualified individuals in a minority group to find lucrative employment. Today the supply of these outstandingly qualified individuals soon disappears, and employers are faced with the requirement and necessity to hire minority members of only average or perhaps even below-average qualifications, who, of course, can be trained. It seems more than likely that the trend of employing increasing quotas of minority workers as a prerequisite for the receipt of a government contract will continue. Indeed, the application of the quota system is likely to widen and to spread into every level of employment. The system manager thus is faced with increasing costs in training programs in order to prepare minority workers adequately for their new responsibilities. This statement is not meant either as a criticism or a complaint but as a fact of the real world which must be faced. The answer is, of course, Be prepared.

OSHA

The Occupational Safety and Health Administration was created in the Department of Labor to promulgate and enforce the provisions of the Williams-Steiger Occupational Safety and Health Act of 1970. However, it is interesting to note that the responsibility for conducting research on which safety and health standards are based lies within the Department of Health, Education and Welfare (HEW). HEW also has the responsibility for implementing educational and training programs through the National Institute for Occupational Safety and Health. A presidentially appointed commission—the Occupational Safety and Health Review Commission—reviews and adjudicates disputes arising from enforcement of the act.

The purpose of the act is "to assure so far as possible every working man and woman in the Nation safe and healthful working conditions and to preserve our human resources."[3] The act also requires OSHA to encourage the states to develop and operate their own job safety and health programs that must be "at least as effective as" the federal program.[4] It attempts to insure that all necessary safety precautions are adopted and enforced in industrial and business facilities, its philosophy being that many employers are unaware of potential hazards; for example, the occasional water drainage—perhaps from a rainstorm—that may accumulate in areas where electrical equipment is used. OSHA inspectors take cognizance not only of modern facilities but also of old, deteriorating, and up until then, unsafe facilities. OSHA inspections cover safety clothing as well as hazard areas, the length of hair as well as the wearing apparel that may constitute a safety hazard under specific working conditions.

It is safe to say that the more society learns about hazardous occupations, the more stringent will OSHA's standards, regulations, and enforcement efforts become. Some industries have recognized hazards—the construction industry, the metal-refining industry, the metal-working

---

3.   Public Law 91-596, 91st Congress, S.2193, December 29, 1970, "Congressional Findings and Purpose," p. 1.
4.   "How OSHA Monitors State Plans," Programs and Policy Series, U.S. Department of Labor, Occupational Safety and Health Administration, January 1975, p. 1.

industry, and the chemical industry, to name but a few. Society is just learning the hazards of the use of nuclear fuel, and this industry will be the subject of much rigorous study to determine specific hazardous occupations and how to reduce the hazards presently perceived.

As a matter of fact, recommendations are currently being made for increased research into safety on a continuing basis, with better standards, more stringent regulations, and improved inspection criteria. OSHA has issued a pamphlet which is "designed to serve as a guide to persons or organizations wishing to comment on OSHA standards."[5] Note the contents of a news item that appeared in a 1975 issue of *Production* magazine. The item reports that changes in OSHA's approach have been suggested as the result of an injury study recently completed by the National Safety Council and the American Society for Testing and Materials. This study analyzed 5,467 injuries and illnesses in six companies operating sixty establishments and employing 40,000 persons. It found that a high percentage of the accidents, many of which were caused by stretching and bending, occurred during the early hours of the workday; that a substantial number of the chemical burns occurred among new employees and on unprotected body areas; and that despite OSHA's frequent citations for National Electrical Code violations, five of the accidents reported involved contact with electrical current. The study indicates a need for greater research into the identified problem areas, revised OSHA inspection criteria, new safety standards, and possible revision of current standards.

OTAF

The Office of Technology Assessment and Forecast, still in its youth, may well have a considerable effect upon business and industry. At least two senses of technology assessment are identifiable. One meaning is that technology assessment is the evaluation of all the potentially harmful effects of a technology. The use of the word "potentially" indicates that a technology, no matter what stage its development, may be banned if it exhibits undesirable effects in the developmental stage—a relatively frequent occurrence. Only consider some of the products of technology of

---

5. "Commenting on OSHA Standards," Programs and Policy Series, U.S. Department of Labor, Occupational Safety and Health Administration, March 1976. Inside cover, "About This Pamphlet."

this century that could well have been banned because of their potentially harmful effects—insecticides, sulfa drugs, coal-fired electric power generation, to name but a few.

The whole question of "potentially harmful" may well become a highly controversial issue in the future. Is it not possible to control (through research efforts) potentially harmful effects in the early development of a technology? Some readers may recall the argument against this country's development of the supersonic passenger-transport aircraft, predicated on the assumption that the flight of supersonic aircraft would be harmful to the ozone layer of the Earth's atmosphere. This damage to the ozone layer would, in turn, permit so much ultraviolet light to penetrate the Earth's atmosphere that human beings would become more susceptible to skin cancer. The fact that this country had, and has had, a number of military aircraft capable of flying at supersonic speeds—and doing so with regularity—was apparently overlooked. How can we determine a "potentially harmful" effect to be real—or just so perceived? At one time, the sound barrier was considered the upper limit on the speed of aircraft. And it was—as long as the aircraft were propeller-driven. With the substitution of the jet engine as the power source for aircraft, passage through the speed of sound became commonplace.

It is arguable that American society would be considerably less affluent and less advanced today if we had foreseen the danger of harmful side effects and had sought to ban some of the then new technologies or products. One possible reaction to the banning of not fully developed technologies exhibiting potentially harmful effects might well be the reduction of business- and industry-funded research and development programs. And, should this come to pass, it is possible that the function of research and development might well come to rest in the federal government, subject to the vagaries of the political and economic climate. Should the United States lose the technological advantage it now enjoys, the markets of Europe and Japan, and the potential markets of China and the Soviet Union, might also well be lost.

The opportunity for OTAF to adopt an optimistic stance is bright. If the second sense of technology assessment is considered the search for optimization, then OTAF may well assess the return expected as well as the risks involved in the adoption of a new technology, and the decision for approval will be made accordingly.

To recapitulate, as long as our society exhibits the safety- and security-consciousness now prevalent, the regulatory agencies will continue to grow in number, strength, and influence. And this is a fact of life that the system manager must take into account.

We have yet to acquire the capability of forecasting specific political developments. Nevertheless, the system manager who is aware of current trends in the social and economic sphere, may better plan for a surprise-free, successful future.

THE INFLUENCE OF MULTINATIONAL CORPORATIONS

Because multinational corporations are growing in both number and influence, they have lately been receiving an increasing amount of attention. Some findings from a searching examination into this fascinating subject are reported below.

The power to shape our daily lives lies increasingly in the hands of executives of global corporations, and there is every reason to believe that these corporations will supplant the nation-state as the most powerful force in our lives and as the major factor in the international system (Barnet and Muller). Richard J. Barnet and Ronald E. Muller report that the multinationals are becoming more and more independent centers of enormous political power, and that in the process, these world managers are undermining the ability of legitimate governments everywhere to bring about necessary social change.

The power of the global corporation derives from its unique capacity to use huge financial resources, pooled technology, and advanced marketing skills to integrate production on a worldwide scale. This exercise of power raises fundamental issues about conflicting loyalties; the refusal of Exxon, for example, to sell oil to the United States Navy, because its overriding interests were to cooperate with the Arab boycott, dramatizes the reality that Exxon is a global company with loyalties that transcend the territory of the United States (Barnet and Muller).

The following failings of the multinational corporation are cited by Barnet and Muller:

1. Multinational corporations attempt to reduce tax liabilities—a strategy in opposition to our national objective of protecting the tax base.

2. Conflict between the global objectives of multinational corporations and the national objectives of underdeveloped countries is evident.

3. Multinational corporations maximize profits at the expense of the weak economies of underdeveloped nations.

4. Multinational corporations do not finance operations in underdeveloped countries with local capital or reinvested earnings but preempt scarce local resources.

5. Much of the technology transferred to underdeveloped countries is overvalued and labor-saving, aggravating local unemployment.

6. The importance of the manufacturing sector to the Latin American economy has increased dramatically, but it employs a smaller percentage of the total work force than it did fifty years ago.

The report concludes that, despite the efforts of some international conglomerates to make positive contributions to poor economies, the net aggregate impact has been negative; it cites the example of Brazil, where the economic miracle wrought largely by global corporations has left the poor poorer.

The shortcomings of today's multinationals have been expertly highlighted. The task of the system manager and of the managers of tomorrow's international conglomerates is to profit from the mistakes of the past and formulate plans to overcome them.

THE ECONOMIC SCENARIO

The economic scenario may be introduced by commenting on a few of the many important areas of interest to economists.[6] Let us consider output, inflation, and energy as representing three of the areas of great concern to our society at this time. The National Planning Association makes periodic projections of the national economy, which serve as very valuable tools in the development of any economic scenario. The information discussed below is synthesized from information in these reports.

The industrial structure of civilian employment in the United States has changed over the past two decades and the same observable trends are expected to continue into the future. Employment in agriculture, for example, which dropped from 7 percent of the national work force in 1960 to about 3 percent in 1975, is expected to have dropped to 1.5 percent by the year 2000. Employment in manufacturing in 1960 represented 25 percent of the work force; it dropped slightly to 24 percent in 1975, and is expected to have dropped to 19 percent in the year 2000. On the other hand, employment in such services as health, entertainment, and tourism, which represented about 17 percent in 1960, increased to almost 20 percent in 1975 and is expected to increase to almost 24 percent by the year 2000. Thirteen percent of the civilian labor force in 1960 was

---

6. The economic scenario is based on a paper, "The Economic Scenario," presented by Mark Fabrycy, Chairman, Department of Economics, and Professor of Economics, Wright State University, at Technological Forecasting Conferences, American Management Associations Center, Chicago, Illinois, December 1974 and May 1975. The scenario was updated in September 1979.

employed in federal, state, and local government. This percentage increased to 18 in 1975 and is forecast to increase to about 25.5 percent by the year 2000.

The system manager who knows what the long-term employment forecast is in a given industry is in a better position to plan for a stable labor force than those who are ignorant of this outlook.

OUTPUT

Considerable changes in the relative importance of various sectors of the economy must be expected. We have noted that the percentage of the labor force in agriculture and manufacturing is expected to decline, while that in services and government will increase. By 1990, the prediction is that federal, state, and local government will be the largest employer of the labor force—with about 23.5 percent of the total. Services, health, entertainment, and tourism will be the second largest employer with an estimated 22.5 percent; and manufacturing will have slipped to the third largest employer with almost 21 percent, compared to its number one standing of nearly 25.5 percent in 1960. These trends are the result of two factors. First, as productivity and per capita income increase, the proportion of income spent on commodities declines, while the proportion spent on services increases. Second, productivity in the production of commodities increases steadily over time, releasing resources for other use. Productivity in most services, on the other hand, increases but little or not at all. Thus, a relative transfer of labor from the commodities sector to the service sector is inevitable.

Total output in the United States grew from 1950 to 1970 at an average annual rate of approximately 4 percent. This growth in output was accompanied by a growth in population over the same period of about 1.25 percent. During the period from 1950 to 1960, our economy experienced a relatively slow rate of saving and domestic gross capital accumulation, amounting to 17 percent of the total Gross National Product (Gutmann, 1965).

To put this concept of investment and growth into its proper perspective, during the previous decade, 1950-1960, the United States ranked seventh in the nations of the world when comparing gross investment as a percentage of the Gross National Product; Japan led with 35 percent, followed by the Soviet Union, West Germany, Italy, France, the United Kingdom, and then the United States with 17 percent (Gutmann, 1965). During this same decade, Japan led the other countries of the world with growth approximating 9 percent of the Gross National Product, with the United States in sixth place with a growth of not quite 3.5 percent in the Gross National Product.

The rate of saving and of domestic capital accumulation is very important in determining the rate of growth of productivity. The rate of growth of the United States population has slowed perceptibly, and it seems probable that by the year 2000, the rate will be zero, with a total population of approximately 300 million persons. This decline in the rate of population growth will in all likelihood be associated with an increase in the labor participation rate and a gradual reduction in the unemployment rate, once the severe slump in the automobile and associated industries, attributed to the energy crisis, has been righted. The United States labor force is expected to continue to grow at a rate of about 1 percent per year. In view of the relatively low rate of gross domestic capital accumulation, it is not expected that productivity will increase rapidly. In fact, powerful competition from the productive areas of Europe and Japan is being presently experienced, and by the late 1980s and early 1990s the expectation is that strong competition will be felt from the large productive areas of the Soviet Union and even of China.

The shift of labor employed in agriculture and manufacturing to the service area will result in a relative decline in the proportion of total output produced by agriculture and manufacturing, and a relative increase in the proportion of total output attributed to services. But while agriculture and manufacturing benefit from increasing returns to scale, services do not possess this attribute. Hence it is expected that the shift toward services will tend to slow the growth of total productivity.

Whereas growth of total output experienced a 4 percent annual growth rate in the period from 1950 to 1970, the expectation is that the period from 1970 to 1990 will see a diminution of the growth rate, and even a decline, to a growth rate approximating 1.25 percent for the decade 1990 to 2000. The reason for this rather dismal forecast is that the annual growth rate approximates 1 percent at present and, with an anticipated zero population growth by the year 2000, and a zero percent labor growth, there is no place to go. Approximately 50 percent of the women in the United States are in the labor force today. The assumption is that very nearly all the women who can and want to go into the labor force are already there.

The United States has a pure technological advance or growth rate of approximately 1 percent annually, compared with a 3.5 percent growth rate (technological) in West Germany and Japan. The growth rate due to investment of capital will be inconsequential. Capital is leaving the United States at the present time. Japan subsidizes investment by building pilot plants for the production of innovative products. The Japanese government —not the inventor and not the entrepreneur—bears the risk of failure for a new product. There is good reason to assume that there will be no massive government interference in the economic process. The subsidy to Japanese inventors and entrepreneurs is perceived as government subsidy to investment. Perhaps government subsidy to investment, by some means not too fettered, is a desirable way to encourage research and development.

For the system manager who is dependent upon large sums of money for validating and developing programs, the outlook is not promising. The cost of developing a major system today is so great that very few corporations can afford the endeavor—without government assistance. The system manager of future years will be required to justify, in great detail and with great confidence, the development of new systems.

INFLATION

Recent experiences with rapidly increasing rates of unemployment, double-digit rates of inflation, and diminishing rates of growth indicate that the United States economy has no effective mechanism to produce simultaneously acceptable levels of employment, inflation, and growth. The mounting political and economic pressures seem to force us toward perhaps our only remaining alternative; that is, a national incomes policy, probably associated with indicative planning.

National incomes policy is an agreement between the national government, labor unions, and the business and industrial community to hold increases in average wage rates, profit rates, and prices to specified levels in order to prevent excessive inflation. Indicative planning relies on business and industrial management to fulfill the elaborate economic forecasts of a central planning agency. Such a plan or operation is further reinforced by the actions and policies of publicly owned industries. France is an example of a nation which has experimented—and successfully so—with indicative planning. Until now, incomes policy has not proved very successful in democratic economies, probably due to the fact that governments in such economies appear to lack the political power to adopt and enforce such a national policy. Indicative planning is voluntary. It seems, however, to mean the apportionment of a given market between the companies in that industry. France is a democratic country having fewer government controls than we have. The French government owns approximately 25 percent of France's national assets. For our country to have an indicative planning program, the Department of Commerce would require, it appears, a "Pentagon" of product and industry planners.

With the exception of France, which is living successfully within an indicative planning economy, these methods of national incomes policy associated with indicative planning have not been widely applied in

Western Europe, probably because of the inability of its political systems to bring about the necessary compromises between the various sectors of society. Even a Socialist country like Yugoslavia (which is the only Socialist country to have a large import-export sector—thanks to tourism, in which it now ranks with Italy) has not always achieved a compromise and at times has had to accept unemployment rates as high as 9 percent to control inflation. As a matter of interest, it should be remembered that Yugoslavia's agricultural industry is fully nationalized.

Should we as a nation decide to try a system of central planning, we must develop our own methods to achieve an acceptable national incomes policy or indicative planning policy and to determine the necessary compromises. The determination of what to do is not so difficult as the determination of how to do it. Judging by the ability evidenced in the past by national economic and political leaders, it seems reasonable, however, to suggest that as a society we will learn the secrets of greater control and responsiveness in our economy in the not too distant future. It even seems reasonable to suggest that by the early 1990s or the year 2000 our society will have overcome the problem of inflation and perhaps will even have established satisfactory rates of employment and growth. System managers, entrusted with such a large percentage of our national resources, must learn to wield the accompanying economic power with understanding and purpose.

THE ENERGY PROBLEM

The energy needs of the United States have been predicted as shown in Figure 7.1.

Energy demand in the United States is projected to grow at a rate of a little less than 1 percent per year through 1990. In the 1990s there is an indicated rise to 1.6 percent per year with this rate including the significant effect of an expected rapid acceleration in synthetic fuels manufacture. Excluding the energy consumed in synfuels manufacture, the growth rate would be 1.2 percent per year, 1990 to 2000.[7] The reader's attention is invited to the fact that our energy demands grew by about 4.5 percent per year prior to the oil embargo against the United States.

---

7.   This section based on "United States Energy Outlook," *World Energy Outlook,* Exxon Background Series, Exxon Corporation, New York, N.Y. 10020, December 1979, pp. 26-27.

It is expected that large amounts of resources will be invested in energy research as rapidly as wisdom permits and that results of this research will enable the reduction of the cost of energy by 1990. This optimistic prediction is based on the following assumptions: (1) there will be a decease in per capita demand for energy, not due so much to the spiraling costs as to the effects of regulation, including the mandatory increase in the average number of miles per gallon that automobile manufacturers must before long make their fleets of cars maintain. (By the year 2000, the transportation sector of energy users is forecast to contribute nearly half of the total savings of energy use.) (2) there will be some slow substitution of fuels—solar energy will become an increasingly important source, as will nuclear energy; and (3) there will be a per capita saving in energy associated with the continuation of the change from an industrial to a service society.

FIG. 7.1: UNITED STATES ENERGY DEMAND AND SUPPLY SOURCES

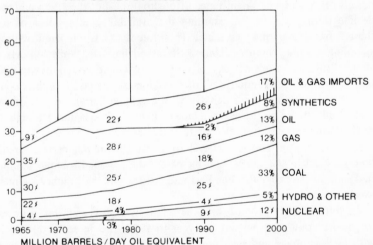

MILLION BARRELS / DAY OIL EQUIVALENT

Source: "World Energy Outlook," Exxon Background Series, Exxon Corporation, New York, N.Y., December 1979, Figure, same title, pg. 27. Used by permission.

Nuclear energy growth is forecast at relatively high rates, 9 percent per year to 1990 then slowing in growth to 4½ percent per year to 2000. Solar energy, by 2000, is projected to be about 200 thousand barrels per day oil equivalent, but this could vary considerably.

Coal is projected to be the largest contributor to energy growth with total production increasing from 7.4 million barrels per day oil equivalent in 1978 to over 20 million barrels per day oil equivalent by 2000. Coal consumption, excluding that related to synfuels production (output and losses), is projected to rise from about 600 million short tons in 1978 to 1 billion tons in 1990 and 1½ billion tons in 2000.

Natural gas production is projected to decline. Domestic oil production is projected to gradually decline from its current level of 10.3 million barrels per day, including natural gas liquids, to between 6 and 6½ million barrels per day in the 1990s.

Synthetics manufacture, both from coal and shale oil, is subject to considerable variation, and production levels will have a direct bearing on the level of United States energy imports. Key factors affecting the rate of development of synfuels production include the extent of support provided by federal and local governments, and the perception of competing energy prices by potential investors. Production could range from three-quarters to 1½ million barrels per day oil equivalent by 1990 and from 4 to 6 million barrels per day by 2000.

Oil and gas imports are projected to be within a 9 million to 11 million barrels per day oil equivalent range throughout most of the 1980s and then decline during the 1990s, assuming the availability of supplies of synthetics from coal and oil shale. This forecast was prepared without assuming a policy limit on United States oil imports. While imports of about 9 million barrels per day of oil plus gas would be required in 2000 with a synfuels production level of 4 million barrels per day, they could decline to 7 million barrels per day with 6 million barrels per day of synfuels as illustrated by the hatched area of Figure 7.1. Gas imports included in the figures above are projected to increase from the current .6 million barrels per day oil equivalent level to about 1.5 million barrels per day oil equivalent in the 1990s. This increase includes added volumes of liquefied natural gas from the Far East and Africa, but the primary source is overland supplies from Canada.

In spite of early promise, and the relatively high growth rate foreseen for nuclear power—9 percent per year to 1990—the potential difficulties with nuclear power and solar power make these sources unlikely to be of any significant assistance prior to the year 2000. Because of availability and cost differentials in alternate sources of energy, it has been projected that coal will be heavily relied upon until the year 2000. Attention is invited to the relative costs of energy as set forth in Figure 7.2.

The cost of converting petroleum from shale on a large-scale, commercial basis remains to be determined, but estimates indicate it to be twice as expensive as obtaining petroleum from other sources. The estimates assume that the water resources necessary in large amounts for the shale conversion process will be available—an assumption that does not appear promising at this time.

FIG. 7.2: RELATIVE COST OF ENERGY (1980)

	Price[*] $/mm BTU
Coal	1.67 [A]
Natural Gas	3.41 [A]
Petroleum	3.85 [A]
Liquid Natural Gas (Imported)	5.79 [A]
Solar	6.20 [B]
Sea Power	6.35 [B]
Gasified Coal	7.53 [B]
Nuclear	13.58 [B]

[*]This data incorporates average
transportation cost.

A. Source: Energy User News, 7 East 12
Street, New York, N.Y. 10003, June 9,
1980. Used by permission.
B. Source: Energy Information Office,
Department of Energy, Washington, D.C.,
June 25, 1980.

The Committee for Economic Development is an independent research
and educational organization, consisting of two hundred trustees who
are mostly business executives and educators. It is nonprofit, nonpartisan,
and nonpolitical; its purpose is to propose policies that will help to bring
about steady economic growth with high employment and reasonably
stable prices, increase productivity and living standards, provide greater and
more nearly equal opportunity for every citizen, and improve the quality
of life for all. The Research and Policy Committee of CED issued a report,
Key Elements of a National Strategy, in June 1977. The report emphasizes
that the era of abundant cheap energy is over and that the people of the
United States must face the fact; there will be significant changes in the
mix of energy we use, and every form of energy is going to cost more.
The report further states that it is a matter of profound urgency to build
a national consensus about these basic principles: (1) we must find increased supplies of energy and must practice greater conservation; (2)
we must rely on the market system and its incentives to insure adequate
production, realistic distribution, and equal opportunities for consumption; (3) we must use more coal and nuclear energy; (4) we must begin
now to develop energy technologies for the next century; (5) we must
learn to use available energy sources without harming the environment;
and (6) we must cooperate with other nations of the world.

System managers may well be able to play an important part in achieving these CED principles. Any manager of a system requiring energy input
can analyze the various acceptable sources and emphasize energy management in the design phase. Those system managers who may be directly

involved in energy-production or energy-distribution systems can plan to make their systems as effective as the state of technology will allow. Some system managers may decide to rely on coal or nuclear energy. System managers in the nuclear industry, the solar-energy industry, and in every and any other industry searching for alternate sources of energy will have as their objectives the development of advanced technologies to supplant dependence on fossil fuels. Such system objectives will include the ability to utilize energy without harm to the environment. System managers frequently have the opportunity to contribute to international cooperative efforts. Undoubtedly, in the future these opportunities will be fully exploited.

IMPLICATIONS OF THE ECONOMIC SCENARIO

The implications of the effects of the rate of growth and composition of output, of the effects of inflation and ways to control it, and of the effects of the sudden energy crisis and answers to energy problems depend to a large extent on the interests and background of the analyst. From the information available at the time, it appears that both the relative and absolute size of government will continue to increase, and as it does, so will its influence on economic affairs. Only through central governmental activity can our society achieve price stability accompanied by reasonable rates of employment/unemployment and growth. This observation is, no doubt, presently unacceptable to some—perhaps to many. The suggestion is raised because of the difficulty being experienced at this time in meeting national economic goals. It has been suggested that a study of some central planning activities by other countries, highlighting the difficulties encountered in order later to be able to plan around the problems experienced by others, might show promise. Again, central planning is far from an attractive option to some. There are those economists who believe that our present economic situation is due to too much central planning—or government intervention. This group believes that the Federal Reserve System "fuels" inflation and federal deficits as a result of activities of the Federal Open Market Committee—a committee composed of seven members of the Board of Governors and five regional bank presidents of the Federal Reserve System. Recommendations to buy or sell government securities at various times is the same as "printing money," according to some.

It seems as if governmental activity and support will surely be necessary to provide the very large amount of resources needed for the research and development required to overcome the problems of developing new sources of energy. Government assistance and support will not only be necessary to fund the research and development efforts of private industry, but also to provide industry with sufficiently attractive tax incentives to stimulate investment in such efforts.

The dangers of excessive governmental power are well known. As our government continues to grow to cope with the problems of today and tomorrow, so must we learn to live with big government and learn how to control it more effectively. The future will see a greater number of social problems become political problems, technological problems become social problems, social problems become economic problems, and so forth. As problems become more complex, solutions also become more complex and require more compromise and cooperation by individuals and groups than ever before. As it has been in the past, our society will be faced with a number of perplexing challenges, but again as in the past, our society will regard these challenges as opportunities, working together to achieve solutions and emerging a wiser, more unified, and in every way, far richer nation.

THE TECHNOLOGICAL SCENARIO

It may be more meaningful to the reader if we first consider the technological scenario in relation to the progress already made and the changes and achievements now expected in the engineering profession.[8] Engineering is characterized by the application of science to the "mechanical" problems of interest to society, and change today, as we have seen, is highly visible in areas of technology; therefore, changes in engineering and engineering methodology and achievements will be highly—and, in some cases, spectacularly—visible.

Recent investigations into modern engineering methods have served to emphasize the importance of finding ways to determine performance criteria and how values are assigned to those criteria and evaluated. Another question being examined is how system engineering trade-off studies may be most effectively utilized, and when and in what form data are best provided to an engineering project. Continuing studies are also investigating what factors affect an engineer's approach to problem solving,

---

8.   The technological scenario is based on a paper, "The Technological Scenario," presented by Francis J. Jankowski, Professor of Engineering, Wright State University, at Technological Forecasting Conferences at the American Management Associations Center, Chicago, Illinois, December 1974 and May 1975. The scenario has been updated as necessary.

what factors affect his or her level of performance, involvement, and a number of other related problems of interest to engineering and system managers.

A tentative result of some of these studies indicates that engineers may be classified into two broad categories—serialists and holists. Serialists tend to organize problems into logical sequences or series and to work on one part of a problem at a time. They seem to prefer to receive information and instructions in the same way. The serialist tends to be the orderly individual that traditional thought holds the engineer to be. Holists, on the other hand, tend to look at a problem in its entirety, or as a unit. They see the whole problem at once and are able to realize how apparently unrelated parts may affect each other. The present training of engineers attempts to make all engineers holistic.

The characteristics that make any given person a serialist or a holist seem to be part of the physical and mental makeup of each individual concerned, and therefore, not subject to quick or easy change. Whether or not continuing research will someday prove this hypothesis, and no matter what the bias in the educational process the future engineer receives, practical experience in system management has reinforced the truth of this hypothesis. This hypothetical knowledge is of considerable value to the system manager in selecting engineers as project managers, members of project teams, or of the scheduling and planning team, and in providing short-term engineering assistance to a technical project or problem.

SOME DIRECTIONS OF CHANGE

The present generation has become accustomed to change. Whereas change occurred slowly in past generations, the rapid improvements in technology and quality of life have produced changes in every area—transportation, communications, education, medical care—think, for example, of the development of artificial organs for human use. Social, political, and to a degree, economic changes occur comparatively slowly, but the effects of changes in technology are swiftly visible—space travel, transoceanic television via satellite, nuclear power, the picturephone, the rapidly increasing capabilities of the computer are only a few instances, selected at random. Future developments in the engineering process that seem likely to bring increasing change include the conquest of the size factor—the ability to make items either very large or very small; the increasing sophistication of the aerospace industry; and the increasing impingement of human factors on the engineering process and the completed product.

SIZE

Even a decade ago, an object weighing one million pounds was considered very large, and a force of one million pounds was considered too large to counter. Today the Apollo space craft and launching rocket weigh nearly five million pounds and are lifted off with a thrust approximating seven million pounds of force. Commercial passenger aircraft the size of the Boeing 747 weigh more than half a million pounds and have a capacity for a truly remarkable number of passengers, most airlines selecting a seating arrangement of approximately 350 passengers. It was not many years ago that a small cruise ship carried about the same number of passengers. But even larger aircraft are now being considered and discussed for future development.

There are many examples of designing products to a very small size. Some examples include small hydraulic lines and valves, small motors and small optics. Some highly visible examples of small designed products may be seen in the electronic and microelectronic areas. Integrated circuits have grown smaller and smaller, resulting in the manufacture of the pocket calculator. An integrated circuit, or chip, may approximate a quarter of an inch in size and yet replace the function of six thousand transistors, which in turn replaced the vacuum tube—a device that some readers may still recall. The advantages of such smallness in size include the ability to use many such units in a small space, providing reliability through redundancy, self-checking and testing features, failure indicators, and a great reduction in the cost per function.

CONTRIBUTIONS OF THE COMPUTER

Computers have had a major impact on modern society, so much so that the increasing development and capability of the computer may well be seen as running parallel to the course of our technical progress. Although a number of technologies may be cited as contributing to the extremely rapid technical developments that have taken place since World War II, none can claim a larger share of credit than the computer.

The computer is already changing our social habits through computerized shopping, cashless transactions, and credit-card utilization, which will, no doubt, shortly lead to remote terminals in the home. The computer is presently being utilized to assist in medical diagnosis, to locate sources or supplies of scarce drugs or rare blood types, to plan better utilization of medical and health-care centers, to simulate human brain functions, and carry out numerous other tasks. In fact, researchers are now pondering the question, What do you say to a computer that talks back to you?

The computer has enabled humankind to find the solution to engineering problems that hitherto seemed far too large and complex for anyone to attempt. It can be incorporated into systems as a control unit, can store and retrieve mountains of data, can process data at an incredibly rapid rate, and perform numerous other functions. In nuclear design, without the use of the computer, only the simplest problems can be solved without great effort. Prior to computer application, the more complicated problems were approximated; they then had to be confirmed or solved by scientific experiment. With the application of the computer, the detailed solution to nuclear design problems can be accomplished in a relatively short period of time—somewhere from a few minutes to a few hours. The complexities of a nuclear engineering problem, including the number of variables to be considered, are suggested by Figure 7.3.

FIG. 7.3: COMPLEXITIES OF A NUCLEAR ENGINEERING PROBLEM

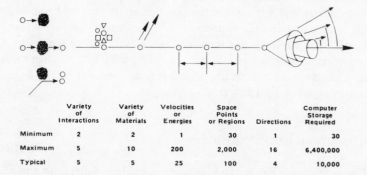

	Variety of Interactions	Variety of Materials	Velocities or Energies	Space Points or Regions	Directions	Computer Storage Required
Minimum	2	2	1	30	1	30
Maximum	5	10	200	2,000	16	6,400,000
Typical	5	5	25	100	4	10,000

Source: Jankowski, F., "The Technological Scenario," an unpublished paper presented at the American Management Associations Technological Forecasting Conference at the Chicago AMA Center, December 3, 1974 (attachment to paper).

The figure affords the reader the opportunity to conceptualize the complexities of a nuclear engineering problem that encompasses five varieties of interactions with five varieties of materials possessing twenty-five velocities or energies, occupying one hundred space points or regions, with particles traveling in four directions, and requiring ten thousand information bits in the computer. Imagine the problem of an engineer faced with the requirement to use ten thousand pieces of hitherto unrelated information. The three astronauts aboard Apollo 13 must have been very grateful that the computer could accommodate the problem—or necessity—of a recalculation of their space trajectory to enable their safe return to Earth after an on-board fire during the outward leg of their journey to the moon.

Thus, the computer lends itself to the design of large systems, permitting interactions to be included and enabling optimization of the system. It is being increasingly applied to data handling, data processing, and many control functions. Computers find application in the numerical control of machine tools, in the traffic control of a city or region, in inventory control, stock control, and control of chemical processes or processing, thereby enabling operations of greater speed and greater scale to be carried out than otherwise would ever be possible.

The computer has revitalized the field of civil engineering. In the 1950s, civil engineers were beset by problems involving calculations of structures too complicated to be done by hand. The computer has now provided the necessary capability.

SOPHISTICATION OF DESIGN

There are usually a number of competing factors to be considered in engineering design. These competing factors include lowness of cost, ease of repair, reliablity, longevity, freedom from sudden catastrophic failure, ease of operation, and maximum performance. They add up to the complexity of determining what possible alternatives there are that will match the desired specifications and achieve the organization's objectives. Until recently, an engineer, in attempting to accommodate the listed demands, would strive for simple rugged products with a preference for manual control. This is exemplified by the effort to replace vacuum tubes with magnetic amplifiers, which are more rugged, less sensitive to shock and vibration, and longer lived than vacuum tubes. The transistor then replaced the magnetic amplifier. More recently, to accommodate consumer demand or preference, and with a view to the competition of the marketplace, the engineer has resorted to a more sophisticated design to take advantage of increased manufacturing capability and to produce more complex products. A case in point is the camera with automated exposure control. This camera produces finished pictures but requires no action on the part of the operator save the aiming of the camera, the focus procedure, and the push of a button. Focusing, the only manual control remaining, may well be automated in the near future.

THE IMPACT OF HUMAN FACTORS

Some very important, though not readily visible, changes in engineering design are the results of the increasing emphasis placed on the incorporation of needs and factors relating to human beings. Some of these factors are of the so-called "ilities"—operability, maintainability, reliability—and product and operator safety. The design engineer is, through the educational process and on-the-job training, being steadily made more aware of the needs of society, the impact of his or her work on society, the effect of the interactions of others on his or her creativity, and the importance of social trends, economic trends, and political trends on his or her efforts, and vice versa.

The modern engineering profession, recognizing the importance of the individual and his or her needs, has established several categories of engineering effort to take into account those needs. One of these categories—human-factors engineering—is concerned with the man-machine-environment system and its interactions, including the limits of operation for a man-machine system, the determination of effective training procedures, and even efforts to determine the desirable characteristics of machine operators. Human-factors engineering has been employed in designing instrument displays for pilots and other aircrew members, for remote control consoles for bank tellers, and in the design of automobiles and even transportation systems.

Safety engineering is the profession's response to the demands of society for protection from potentially harmful products, processes, and operations, and a potentially harmful environment. The safety procedures and practices of industrial corporations affect employees, customer relations, public relations, and the organization's own image, insurance rates, and labor costs. The Occupational Safety and Health Act of 1970 aroused interest and activity in safety engineering. Consumer-interest groups, stimulated by the efforts of Ralph Nader, have continued to demand product safety.

The culmination of these various demands for convenience, safety, and the "ilities" is that design engineers have begun to realize their responsibility for the consequences of their work. Universities, with increasing impetus, are also involving engineering students in courses dealing with social problems and value judgments that introduce problems in which the contributions of the engineer may prove significant. As engineers become more cognizant of these problems, the effect of social needs will become more evident in design processes and products—a desirable effect of the feedback process.

In years past, a licensed engineer was an engineer in direct contact with the public, whose work directly influenced public safety. Most licensed engineers were civil engineers, concerned with the design and construction of buildings, bridges, and highways. Now, however, consumer groups are proposing that engineers who are in any way a part of the design process of, say, an automobile be held accountable for the results of their work.

It appears that the move to require professional licensing of all engineers will soon result in a great increase in the number of those licensed—presently representing approximately 10 to 20 percent of the whole. The National Society of Professional Engineers is an advocate of more rigorous licensing practices. At present, some states are removing the "manufacturing exemption"—which does not require the licensing of engineers engaged in the design of manufactured products. Some states are requiring that all engineering faculty be licensed—not a universal requirement at present. Broadening and strengthening licensing requirements for professional engineers may—like the effects of OSHA—prove more difficult for the small manufacturer than the large one, but it is also likely, as in the case of OSHA, to prove of benefit to society.

ENGINEERING EDUCATION

Today's engineering student, as we have indicated, is finding emphasis placed on making the learning experience more realistic and more relevant to society and society's needs. One approach now in use is the assignment of a project, case study, or problem-solving exercise that lasts throughout the student's entire senior year. Courses in which social problems and social values are weighed along with technical feasiblity are more and more being introduced into engineering colleges. Flexible scheduling, the introduction of more audiovisual aids, and the measurement and reward of effective teaching are additional improvements to be seen in the engineering curriculum. The net effect is to modify the emphasis on the purely technical content of the engineering curriculum and to introduce why, when, and if, as well as how. Future engineers will be equipped to contribute to society in more than just the engineering discipline.

THE ENGINEERING PROCESS OF THE FUTURE

A forecast of the results of the engineering process in the future, based on present trends, is that the size of products will become both far larger and far smaller than is possible now. The ability to form and machine metal parts of greater size than is presently possible will develop. The trend toward miniaturization, subminiaturization, and even subsub-miniaturization will continue. Computers will be used even more extensively in the engineering design process, as well as in the control of mechanical manufacturing processes, in directing the use of products, and as components in a system. Human factors will have an increasingly greater impact on product design and use by the improved matching of machine and operator—including crews—to permit improved operability, maintainability, and reliability. The concept of social responsibility will become more visible in product design. The professional responsibility of engineers will continue to be enhanced by broader licensing requirements. And, finally, the educational process will be enriched and increase the sensitivity of engineering graduates to the concept of social responsibility, to the importance of human factors in the design process, and to better prepare them than even at present to incorporate new knowledge into practical design concepts and techniques.

DISCERNIBLE TRENDS

Business and industry are already aware of the fact that the future must be taken into account. The system manager is aware that he or she can invent the future. The only problem is the usual one—How?

One researcher, investigating the trend of more and more companies seeking to forecast the future in order to plan more adequately for it, has found some interesting examples of these activities, some of which are indicated below (Gallese):

1. The Gillette Company is studying the possible effects of the changing role of women. Another study finds that a stabilized population will need a lesser rate of growth in new products. A possible result is that future growth will come from services, not new products.

2. It is estimated that 1 out of 5 of the "Fortune 500" companies now have technological forecasting executives. Shell Oil Company, the American Telephone and Telegraph Company, and the General Electric Company are among those trying to discern future implications in past and present trends.

3. The General Electric Company saw trends and established affirmative-action guidelines a year before the federal government required them.

4. Mr. Richard Davis, then of the Whirlpool Corporation, forecast the coming of permanent-press fabrics. Whirlpool was the first on the market with washers and dryers that accommodate such materials. Mr. Davis is reported as saying that he relies on social, political, and environmental factors, as well as on technological factors.

All signs point to the fact that system managers must be alert to signals of change, to trends and events that herald change, and to the awareness that changes in social, economic, political, and other environmental factors are fully as important to technological progress as research, science, and engineering. Some relatively recently learned lessons include the experiences of our armed forces in such conflicts as Korea and Vietnam. It has been reported that our forces were geared to a nuclear showdown. When circumstances did not warrant so dire an eventuality, optional plans of a more conventional nature were needed. A look into the future is really valuable only if it considers all possibilities.

8...PLANNING AND CONTROL

INTRODUCTION

The earlier chapters have dealt with the importance of developing a working philosophy of management, of the advantages and disadvantages of the bureaucratic organization, of the effect of conflict, and of the advantages to the system manager of understanding and avoiding conflict situations. Also discussed in the earlier chapters were some important functional areas that should be included in the system management office, the particular importance of configuration management, the potential impact of environmental factors, system objectives and procedures by which to achieve those objectives. This chapter is designed to give the reader an enlarged conceptual view of those fundamental functions of the system manager—planning and control.

One definition of planning is that it is the means by which management determines an acceptable course of action to achieve predetermined objectives with those resources that are available. Note, as was indicated earlier, that no admonition is made to select the best or optimum course of action, which is a matter of personal judgment. The acceptable course of action is to determine which of the alternative plans is most likely to receive the enthusiastic support of all those affected by the plan or responsible for its implementation. No further comment on predetermined objectives is needed. The system manager is well aware of the technical and management objectives which he or she and his or her organization seek to achieve. Additional comment is necessary, however, concerning the resources available. It is hardly worth the time of the system manager to develop plans requiring the expenditure of more resources, personnel, facilities, time, and money than are reasonably and readily available. In extreme cases, it may, of course, be necessary to modify technical and management requirements in order to proceed, with available resources, toward the achievement of system objectives.

Today's system manager might well conceive of the division of the. authority-responsibility relationship as parts of a rectangle halved by a line running diagonally from the lower left-hand corner to the upper right-hand corner. The upper half of the rectangle would then represent the authority that has been delegated to him or her in that particular managerial situation. Authority is the right of decision and command to plan and control the organization's activities, for which the system manager is responsible, toward the achievement of predetermined objectives. Authority has also been defined as the force that allows control of an organization. The incumbent in a position of authority can delegate some of this authority to subordinates as he or she develops confidence in a subordinate and enlarges the subordinate's area of management influence. Delegation of authority, more specifically, is the release of authority to subordinate managers to perform expected functional tasks. The system manager must never delegate authority as a substitute for leadership, nor ask for more authority when, in truth, he or she should be exercising more leadership ability.

The lower half of the conceptualized rectangle may be perceived as the responsibility inherent in the position. Responsibility is the obligation a person incurs for effective completion of an objective at the time a given task is assigned by superior management—or when the person accepts such a position. Responsibility cannot be delegated. Rather, the individual who has been delegated authority assumes the concept of accountability, which is the requirement or condition that the subordinate keeps superior management informed on the discharge of his or her responsibilities. Thus, the concepts of authority and of the delegation of power, of responsibility and accountability, do much to determine the sort of organization a system manager develops. For inasmuch as an organization is the structural and authoritative relationships between persons engaged in group activities toward the achievement of predetermined objectives, management of those relationships has largely to do with these very concepts of authority, responsibility, and accountability.

Today's managerial planners, however, see an explosion in the numbers of variables that must be considered. In 1975 the *Wall Street Journal* reported that, whereas formerly the planning staff of Standard Oil Company of Ohio arrived at a consensus on how the economy would unfold during the planning period and constructed an operating plan to fit that consensus, the consideration of "what-if" questions have required the development of five contingency or "what-if" plans for that year alone. According to the same source, the Chase Manhattan Bank reduced the length of plans in which hard numbers are used to three years, a reduction in time from the five years formerly used.

It is apparent that as the number of variables used in the planning process increases, the consideration of the interactions and interdependencies becomes exponentially difficult. The consideration of such questions as "What if a selected variable changes in value, what will the impact upon other variables be?" will keep planning staffs increasingly busy in the future. The following discussion is intended to familiarize the reader with tools to assist in the planning process.

STEPS IN PLANNING

The objectives—both technical and managerial—of the system are well known by the system manager. The first step, then, in planning is the establishment of premises, which are the set of assumptions concerning the conditions that now exist and are expected to continue to exist throughout the life of the system. Of course, any changes in present trends or any factors that may or are likely to alter existing trends are of utmost importance to the system manager and must be considered. (Some of the factors that may affect present trends have already been discussed in the previous chapter and will again be discussed later in this chapter.)

The determination of premises may best be made by technological forecasting techniques, some of the more effective and popular of which are described below. It is important to the system manager that all subordinate managers in the system organization accept and support the planning premises, once they have been established. Stated another way, it seems ludicrous to assume that enthusiastic support will be forthcoming if subordinate managers and supporting personnel and organizations assume that the future is going to be quite different from what the system manager believes. Plans and procedures need therefore to be established to prevent other participants from second-guessing the system manager's plans and actions.

PREMISES BY TECHNOLOGICAL FORECASTING

Technological forecasting is the prediction or determination of the feasible or desirable characteristics of performance parameters in future technologies (Lanford, 1972). Not every technique of technological forecasting can be applied to every problem, and most experts are unwilling to accept the results achieved by a single method, so that the system manager should remember to apply as many technological forecasting methods as possible to each problem area. Then, if the results attained by most of the methods point in the same direction, the system manager may have some confidence that the overall or integrated forecast is correct and that his or her planning premises are valid.

METHODS OF TECHNOLOGICAL FORECASTING

Technological forecasting requires that the system manager consider the social, political, economic, and environmental consequences of specific functional advances prior to embarking on a full-scale program of change. The consideration of desirable performance in the future allows the manager to work backward from the future to the present, highlighting technical areas not sufficiently developed to attain the desired performance during the planning period. Once these areas are identified and measured, the system manager can allocate resources to these undeveloped functional areas to develop the required technical knowledge.

There does not appear to be any one best starting point for entry into technological forecasting activities. Some managers prefer the contextual map as a starting point, while others prefer fitted curve trend extrapolation, and still others prefer the Delphi technique. In technological forecasting, the initial technique employed is not a critical matter. The search for and the analysis of information often causes the manager to integrate techniques.

System managers are advised to initiate their technological forecast by using a method for which sufficient trained personnel, money, and data are available. Once a forecaster—or group of forecasters—has had success in developing forecasts by a single technique, forecasts developed by combined techniques may be attempted.

Contextual mapping is the process of portraying visually or graphically the progress of a technical area over a period of time. Contextual mapping communicates graphically the evolution of a trend, relates contributing technologies to specific devices, assists in the analysis of causal relationships in the technical progress, and allows the projection of future progress in the technical area of interest. Contextual mapping has the additional advantage of indicating parameters of interest for forecasts of the future.

The development of a contextual map may begin with a recognized work in the technical area to develop a visual presentation of the history of the development of the parameter of interest. Figure 8.1 shows the development of such a map.

FIG. 8.1: DEVELOPMENT OF A CONTEXTUAL MAP

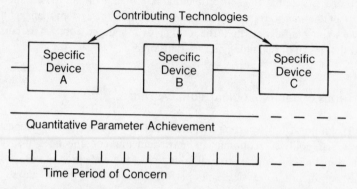

Source: H. W. Lanford and L. V. Imundo, "Approaches to Technological Forecasting as a Planning Tool," "Long Range Planning," Vol. 7, No. 4, August 1974, Fig. 1, p. 49.

FIG. 8.2: TREND EXTRAPOLATION

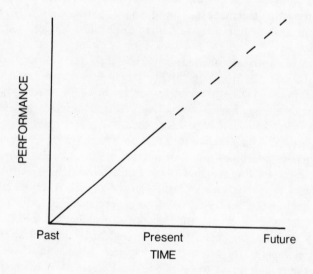

FIG. 8.3: TREND EXTRAPOLATION BY FITTED CURVE

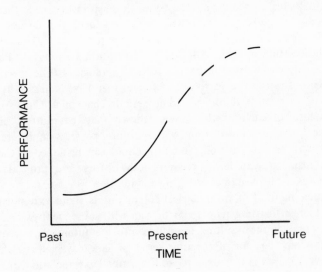

**FIG. 8.4: DEVELOPMENT OF AN ENVELOPE CURVE
TO SHOW AN EXTRAPOLATION**

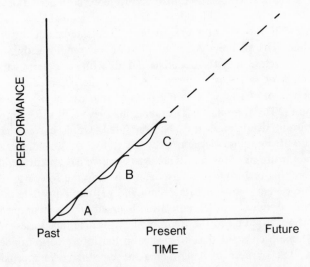

A horizontal line on the chart may be subdivided into whatever time periods are convenient. A second line parallel to the first may be added to indicate quantitative performance of the parameter in question. A third line with boxes containing the names of those specific devices that have produced the performances noted may be added, the devices being generally vertically above the corresponding performance figures achieved in applicable time periods. A fourth line of information may be inserted above to show associated or contributing technologies to the specific devices demonstrated. The performance figures may have increased by some orders of magnitude during the time periods concerned. Curves of the performance of each of the devices shown may be plotted, and an envelope curve developed from which future progress in future time periods may be extrapolated. This projection may be added to the contextual map to graphically present both history and projections of progress—as the broken lines of the figure indicate.

Another method of technological forecasting is trend extrapolation—the plot of an existing time series of data with subsequent extension or extrapolation of the resulting trend line into the future. The trend line resulting from the plot of the time series of data may be a straight line or a curve. Figure 8.2 is an example of linear trend extrapolation.

The past data points are plotted to the present time, and an extrapolation extended into the future. The expected performance for a future time period may be read directly from the extrapolation. A general rule of thumb is that the extrapolation into the future covers a period of time no longer than that for which historical data points are available.

All data will not present a straight line. When the data do not follow a straight line, either directly or by plotting on semilogarithmic paper of various cycles, the forecaster is faced with a determination of what formula or relationship most closely fits the observed data points. The objective, of course, is to find a formula that can be used for predictive purposes. The formula for a parabola may give a fit sufficiently close so that future data points may be computed. Other curves that have proved useful are those developed by Pearl for use in biology and by Gompertz for use in economics. The logistics curve has also proved useful. So relationships or formulae are available whereby the forecaster can (1) fit the line or curve to the data points and (2) compute data points in future time periods. Trend extrapolation is based on the assumption that the factors contributing to the trend of the historical time series are more likely to remain constant than to change in the future period under consideration. The purpose of determining the type of curve approximated by the plot of the time-series data is the selection of the proper formula with which to compute and plot future points. The key to development of trend extrapolation is the development and use of time-series data tables. Data may be derived from government publications, trade association data, internal sources, university business and economic centers, and research agencies. Figure 8.3 shows a curve developed from a logistics curve formula.

Examination of the plot of the data points led the forecaster to believe that a logistics curve would fit the data. Application of the logistics curve formula produced usable results, and future points were computed by the same formula. It is possible that several curve formulae will be tried before one is found that produces an acceptable result. The selection of the curve formula is a personal decision, and it is quite possible that no formula can be found to produce acceptable results, in which case the trend extrapolation method cannot be used.

Technological progress in many functional areas has shown exponential progress, or progress in conformance with the familiar S-shaped curve. This curve indicates that progress measured in terms of performance is relatively slow upon introduction of the innovation, accelerates upon acceptance, and slows again as the device or process approaches maturity and is being replaced by a superior technology.

The envelope curve technique is the plotting of the performance achieved by several succeeding technologies on the same time and performance graph. The S-shaped curves of each succeeding technology or device may be joined by a tangential straight line or smoothed curve to indicate what the overall past progress has been, and the line or curve projected or extrapolated to indicate what future performance is expected in time periods of interest. Figure 8.4 shows the development of an envelope curve.

In Figure 8.4 we note the functional performance of three devices, all performing the same function, with B replacing A and C replacing B, through time. The first device under consideration—A—exhibits progress in conformance with the S curve—relatively slow progress in development, more rapid progress during the period of acceptance and widespread use, and a declining rate of progress, followed by leveling of the rate of progress, and eventual replacement by device B. Device B follows the same life cycle and is eventually replaced by device C. A point on the curve of the development of devices A, B, and C may be selected and joined by a straight line, if appropriate, or by a curve, if necessary or desired. An extrapolation of the line or curve may be made to show what progress may be expected in the future by some perhaps still-unnamed device to be developed.

The development of the laser serves well to demonstrate the envelope curve technique. The frequency spectrum has been steadily extended by a number of devices whose specific performances may be plotted as a series of familiar S curves and a line tangent to the various S curves projected into future time periods to indicate expected performance. Figure 8.5 illustrates the performance of devices leading to the laser. The data to plot Figure 8.5 were developed from the work of a researcher in the laser field (Eaglesfield).

FIG. 8.5:   APPLICATION OF THE ENVELOPE CURVE
              TO THE DEVELOPMENT OF THE LASER

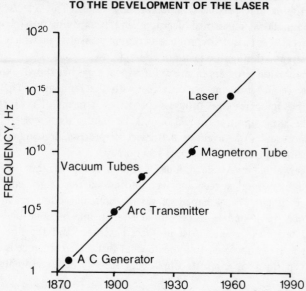

The DC generator and the AC generator were early steps in the development of the laser, or in the extension of the frequency spectrum. The first device considered in this demonstration is, however, the arc transmitter, whose developmental life cycle followed the S curve. The vacuum-tube life cycle followed the S curve, as did the magnetron and as does the laser. A straight line was drawn roughly through tangential points of the S curve of the arc transmitter, the vacuum tube, the magnetron tube, and the laser, and an extrapolation of the straight line formed was made into the future to see what performance might be expected. As a matter of interest, patents were issued in 1975 for lasing materials that will already permit the frequencies forecast for the decade 1990 and the year 2000.

Another method used in technological forecasting is the substitution phenomenon or effect. The substitution effect is premised on the belief that one product or technology that exhibits a relative increase in performance over an established or conventional product or technology will eventually replace the product or technology of lesser performance. Once such substitution has begun, it will continue to completion. Figure 8.6 shows the development of a substitution curve.

FIG. 8.6:   A SUBSTITUTION CURVE

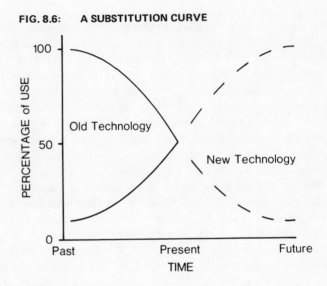

This figure displays graphically the substitution of one device or process for another. When as little as 2 percent take-over of the market or usage of the new technology has been noted, the time period during which the new technology will take over 50 percent of the market or usage can be fairly accurately determined. Once the new technology has taken over 20 percent of the market, the time period during which the new technology will take over 100 percent of the market can be accurately projected, assuming no major wars or economic depressions.

Trend extrapolation or envelope curves may also be used in the development of lines and curves showing the phasing out of old technology and its eventual replacement by new.

In a study of water-pollution control procedures and progress, an effort was undertaken to determine the percentage of municipalities possessing sewage-treatment facilities that had converted from primary to secondary treatment methods, the secondary technique being a more advanced and more effective one. From the data obtained, the substitution-effect technique was employed to determine at what point the secondary-treatment technique would completely replace the primary technique, or to determine what factors would prevent or slow this substitution. The beginning date was 1900, the 50 percent take-over point was reached in 1935, and the 100 percent point (or total take-over) projected to be 1990. In the plot of this particular curve, it was necessary or desirable to smooth out perturbations appearing in the period from 1930 to 1940 (the economic depression of the 1930s) and the period from 1940 to 1946 (World War II).

When data points are plotted graphically, and the curve appears to follow the S-shaped pattern, it has been pointed out that the forecaster may choose to use a relationship or formula developed for use in some other discipline for predicting future data points. A curve that was developed to predict biological growth may be used if the data show the initial advance to be exponential, where the curve is symmetrical to the inflection point, and where the rate of progress diminishes as it approaches an upper, perceived limit (Pearl, 1924). The upper limit may be a presently perceived physical limit, as the speed of sound was once perceived to be the limit of aircraft speed.

An earlier study generated data concerning the manufacture and use of synthetic fiber. To produce a forecast of the time period in which all fiber being manufactured and used would be synthetic, Pearl's Law was employed. The curve was first plotted from observed or historical data. From an examination of the resulting curve, the decision was made to plot the extrapolation by analogy to Pearl's Law. The extrapolation by this method indicates that by the year 2000, synthetic fiber will have reached 100 percent and taken over the entire market.

Another formula, developed to model economic growth, may be used if the data show the initial advance to be exponential—where the curve is not symmetrical to an inflection point, and where the rate of progress shows continuous diminution as it approaches an upper perceived physical limit (Gompertz, reported by Kuznets, 1930).

In an earlier study on the development and projected use of the artificial heart by human beings, it was subjectively decided, after an examination of the plot of available data, to apply Gompertz' Law to the generated data. (The reader's attention is directed to the fact that no historical data were available.) The forecast of the number of artificial hearts needed in future time periods, as determined by an analogy to Gompertz' Law, indicates that in 1980 some usages will appear and that such demand will increase rather rapidly until a saturation point for the need or for legitimate applications of the artificial heart in humans is reached in the year 2005, and will remain thereafter relatively constant at the rate of 180,000 implantations per year. It should be well understood that the assumptions made and the perceived upper limit and its method of derivation influence the results of a projection by analogy. Attention is again directed to the fact that no historical data exist for this projection. Purely personal decisions were made in selecting the beginning date and determining the upper limit used in the model.

There are times when the pattern of progress of a later technology follows the pattern or curve of progress of an earlier technology but is separated by a time lag. As long as the curve of progress of the later technology parallels the curve of progress of the earlier precursive one, the "leader-follower" relationship is useful.

In the past, it was believed that only technical progress could serve as a precursor; recent research, however, indicates that economic, political, and social factors may also. Although it is difficult to determine precursive indicators, the discovery of one adds to the confidence of the forecaster in his overall results. The development of a precursive indicator curve is shown in Figure 8.7.

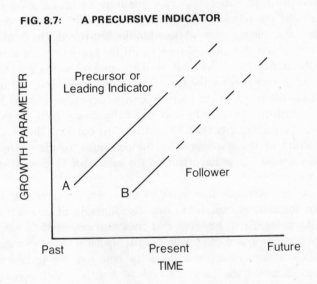

FIG. 8.7:   A PRECURSIVE INDICATOR

Note that the progress of curve A—or device A—is plotted in a time period earlier than that of curve B—or the progress of device B. (The straight line is a special curve belonging to a family of simple polynomials expressed as

$$y_t = a + bx + cx^2 + dx^3 + ex^4 + \ldots$$

where all constants beyond *b* are zero.) Curve *B* is roughly parallel to curve *A*. If a study of the two curves or devices leads the forecaster to believe that their progress is dependent upon or influenced by the same set of circumstances or environment, then a forecast of device *B* can be made by projecting the historical curve of *B* into the future, parallel with the curve of progress of device *A*. A very popular demonstration of this technique is that of the speed trend of commercial passenger aircraft following the speed trend of military transport aircraft by a time lag of from eleven to thirteen years.

A popular method of forecasting technology is the Delphi technique. The Delphi method of forecasting involves the use of a questionnaire asking selected experts in many fields to name the approximate time period when they expect some specified events to occur. A systematic solicitation of expert opinion works toward a consensus by the use of sequential interrogations. Following receipt of the responses to the first survey, the individual or organization conducting the survey prepares a second questionnaire giving the results of the first survey, and asking those who provided responses outside the interquartile range—or middle 50 percent of the responses—to give reasons why their answers departed from the consensus responses obtained in the first round. The third round of the survey provides all participants with the justification or reasoning behind the extreme answers; that is, those answers which are at either end of the distribution for the time frame being considered, and outside the interquartile range. In the fourth round, which occurs after all participants have had the opportunity to consider the reasons given for extreme positions, the participants are asked for one last opinion. The reason for the departure of the response from the consensus, or the interquartile range of responses, is as important to the researcher as the statistically mean responses.

The Delphi technique thus provides the individual forecaster with a consensus forecast, by experts in many disciplines, in an area of interest. It must be pointed out, however, that consensus responses do not occur for every question posed or opinion sought; bipolar responses are received to certain questions. If a consensus is the objective, the researcher can choose to disregard the second round of questions and rephrase the original questionnaire in a manner designed to achieve a consensus, or develop a rationale for the bipolarity of the responses.

An integrated scenario of the future may be compared to a science-fiction novel or movie concerning some future time period—as already discussed in Chapter 7. Scenario development is effective in developing a broad base of knowledge to facilitate an understanding of major factor relationships; it is an important technique to be integrated with other approaches to technological forecasting. In effect, the scenario becomes the basis for planning premises of the future.

Yet another interesting technique to generate knowledge of the future is the cross-impact technique. The cross-impact technique determines the relevance and strength of relevance between events that are forecast to occur in the future. This technique determines whether the occurrence of one event, which is forecast, will enhance or inhibit the probability that each of the other specific events forecast will occur.

Olaf Helmer and Ted Gordon have provided an outline of the steps that must be taken in order to develop a cross-impact analysis. These steps, modified by Helmer and Gordon from steps proposed by the researchers who originated the cross-impact concept, are as follows: (1) Choose a forecast event and subjectively determine its probability of occurrence; (2) Assume that the first event occurs. Determine the probability of occurrence of each of the other forecast events. Does the occurrence of the first event enhance or inhibit the probability of occurrence of each of the other forecast events? (3) Perform the same exercise on each of the other events. In turn, each of the events being considered becomes the "first" event and probabilities of other events are determined *should* this first event occur; and (4) Using a computer, compute the matrix a number of times to determine probabilities of occurrence. The number or percentage of times an event occurs during the repeated exercises will help to determine its probability of occurrence.

To develop a cross-impact matrix exercise, a listing of each event considered in the economic, social, political, and general technological area should be made. For early exercises, it is suggested that a small number of events, say three, be considered in each area. A number is assigned each event, from top to bottom of the listing. The future year by which some predetermined probability of occurrence—say 60 percent—is expected is listed for each event, and the probability of occurrence in some predetermined time period—say the year 2000—subjectively assigned. The events listed are those events used in a Delphi questionnaire or exercise. Questions may be developed to determine when a certain probability—say 60 percent—of occurrence is expected. They may also be developed to show the probability of occurrence by a certain year—say 2000—that is expected by the Delphi respondents. This procedure represents one technique of obtaining initial probabilities and probabilities by a certain year.

From the event listing just discussed, the forecaster may subjectively determine on his or her own or by group consensus what the impact on all other events will be if event one comes to pass. A cross-impact matrix should be developed listing events one through twelve down the list from top to bottom, and across the top of the list from left to right. A technique suggested for early exercises is to go through the matrix the first time assigning only plus and minus signs and zero, to indicate the direction of impact on other events, should the event under consideration occur. A second review of the matrix can then be used to assign numbers indicating the relative strength of the impact or relationship. Again, this can be accomplished by a single forecaster or by a group of individuals seeking consensus opinions. Each event, one through twelve, is considered, with the event's impact on all other events. The numbers representing strengths of impact may run from plus ten through zero to minus ten, or from plus four through zero to minus four, or whatever scale a specific organization chooses to use.

For illustrative purposes, assume that the economic scenario will develop the following three points, in addition to others: (1) there will be a leveling in the percentage of the United States Gross National Product (GNP) spent on health care; (2) poverty will essentially be eliminated; and (3) there will be a decrease in the percent of the GNP spent on medical research.

Then assume that the political scenario or a Delphi questionnaire results in the following premises, again in addition to others: (1) increased government participation in family life; (2) an increased demand for artificial organs; and (3) government regulation of health care—something like the present utilities commission.

Further assume that the social scenario results in the following premises, again in addition to others: (1) changes in the provision of health care services; (2) the establishment of national health insurance; and (3) an increase in the number of artifical organ implants desired.

Accepting all these premises, the application of the cross-impact matrix technique will allow the consideration of potential impact on other events, should one of the forecast events occur.

The cross-impact matrix requires the detailed consideration of the effects of potential interactions among the different individual events that are forecast to occur. The cross-impact method requires the determination of the potential impact of one of the forecast events, should it occur, on each of the other forecast events. The cross-impact effect may be positive if the occurrence of the event forecast will enhance the probability that the other forecast events will occur. The cross-impact effect may be negative if the occurrence of the forecast event will inhibit the probability of the occurrence of the other events forecast. Weights may be assigned to indicate relative or comparative strengths of the belief that the occurrence of one forecast event will either enhance or inhibit the probability of the occurrence of the other forecast events.

Once the cross-impact matrix has been reduced to plus, zero, or minus for all relationships, showing the assumed initial probabilities of occurrence—the estimated years until the occurence—then the probabilities of all events may be calculated by the equation shown in Figure 8.8 (Helmer and Gordon):

FIG. 8.8:   CALCULATION OF CROSS IMPACT PROBABILITIES

$$p_n^1 = \frac{S}{10}\left(\frac{t-tm}{t}\right)p_n^2 + \left[1 - \frac{X}{10}\left(\frac{t-tm}{t}\right)\right]P_n$$

P_n is the probability of occurence which event n had prior to the occurence of event m.

p_n^1 is the probability of occurence which event n has after the occurence of event m.

S is the number from $+10$ to -10 which is a measure of the mode and strength of the cross-impact of event m on event n.

t is the number of years to the date in the future for which the probabilities are being estimated.

tm is the number of years to a date in·the future when event m is assumed to have occured.

Source: Extracted from paper "Generation of Internally Consistent Scenarios through the Study of Cross-Impact", Olaf Helmer & Ted Gordon.

A computer is an invaluable asset, if not a necessity, in the determination of probabilities. Attention is again invited to the fact that, for illustrative purposes only, a relatively small number of possible events have been selected. Some organizations work with a matrix of 90 events, or 8,100 relationships.

A refinement of the scenario is the Relevance Tree or Perspective's Tree. In developing a Relevance Tree, major factors affecting the problem under investigation are functionally arranged. Every subfactor relevant to the major factors is then listed and catalogued under its respective major factor. The Relevance Tree, as developed by Battelle Columbus Laboratories, is commonly constructed of three major sections—or domains: environmental, utilities and functions, and technical. The environmental domain includes all possible environmental factors—political, social, economic, and technical—that may have an impact on the subject under investigation; the domain of utilities and functions represents all uses, functions, and consumer demands that are relevant to a particular investigation; and the technical domain portrays as nearly as possible all alternative technical paths or methods—electrical, hydraulic, pneumatic, manual—and combinations of paths or possibilities to achieve the desired utility, function, or technical objective.

Once all factors that can be discovered or identified by the forecaster have been listed and catalogued under similar or related subgroupings, the Relevance Tree is developed by graphically linking each factor in the environmental group to a factor (or to each of those factors) in the functions and utilities or the technical domain by which it may be related or affected. The next step is to relate each competing or alternative technology that can fulfill the requirements of the functional objective to each of the factors in the functional group that will or do represent the objective. The end result is a graphical representation of the many environmental factors bearing on the achievement of the end-use attributes or functional objectives, together with a visual presentation of all possible technical systems or combinations of technologies that can achieve the objective.

In a study of the future expected for the industrial robot, a Relevance Tree was developed that listed in the environmental domain, social, political, economic, and general technological factors. Some factors listed in the social area included the decreased motivation to perform undesirable types of work, the adoption of a behavioralist management philosophy, and the workers' increased self-esteem. Some of the listed political factors included enforcement of OSHA regulations, involvement in foreign wars, and government support of related research and development. Some factors listed in the economic area included the increased cost of labor, the decreasing cost of industrial robots, and the increased domestic and international competition. Some factors listed in the general technological area included advances in artificial intelligence, advances in optical processing, and advances in motive sources.

The utilities and functions domain included utility factors and functional factors and the technical objective. Utility factors listed included increased productivity, decreased unit costs, and decreased employee turnover. Functional factors listed included flexible automation, improved product quality, and better working conditions; the utilities and functions domain showed the product linked upward with factors from the environmental domain and downward with factors in the technical domain.

The technical domain included such factors as controllers of position resolution (mini-computers, core memory, and semiconductor devices), controllers of motive sources (hydraulic, electrical servos, and electrical motors), sensors for adaptive control (both visual and tactile), and materials.

Lines of relevance between related factors may be drawn. The reader will observe the wide variety of factors, listed by different individuals or organizations, that may be of interest. The lines of relevance also represent subjective decisions.

A fully developed Relevance Tree serves as a valuable tool in forecasting and in long-range planning.

THE DEVELOPMENT OF ALTERNATIVE COURSES OF ACTION

One alternative course of action is, of course, to do nothing. It will, however, be a rare occurrence when the system manager chooses this alternative. Perhaps, the greatest single error made in planning is the selection of the first developed course of action. With the availability of the computer, the system manager is able to work out in detail a large number of complete alternatives. Armed with this technically developed plan, the system manager, versed in theory and practice of organizational behavior, may predict the behavior or support of those responsible for implementing the plan. Should the predicted behavior not be desirable or acceptable, other alternatives should be considered, in which case the system manager should select a technically acceptable alternative that all concerned will enthusiastically endorse and implement.

Once the plan has been selected, the system manager will organize around areas of expected results and around the effective supervisors available. As emphasized in Chapter 1, in planning the organization structure and the subsequent staffing of the structure, a trade-off process of what effective supervisors are available to manage what functions, combined with the system manager's conceptualization of authority and communication, must be accomplished.

LESSONS LEARNED FROM PAST EXPERIENCE

The past experience of system managers of large and complex systems indicates that the time and effort spent in the conceptual phase of the system life cycle is time and effort well spent. The results of the year or two devoted to planning effort, involving studies to insure that the system concept under consideration is technically feasible and that the effectiveness of the planned system will justify the cost, and identifying the preferred alternative or alternatives to achieve the system objectives, cannot be overemphasized. The planning effort of the conceptual phase identifies all technical concepts, required manpower, facilities, and other resources;

it highlights new technologies requiring investigation and exploitation, indicates areas of expected difficulty, and assesses the technical and management risks involved. The conceptual phase results in the development of a functional base line for the system and its subsystems and the identification of subsystems or items requiring a long lead time to develop and manufacture. The manpower resources of perhaps thirty to forty persons to supervise these conceptual studies is a necessary investment for the manager of a large and complex system.

The work of the conceptual phase should result in the acceptance of a clearly defined life cycle, with development risks, schedules, and funding requirements understood and accepted by all participants, so that system life-cycle redirection will be held to a minimum.

One of the lessons learned from experience is that the utilization of the first complete system as a means of developing manufacturing techniques or a subsystems developmental test bed can lead to inefficient, time-consuming, and complicated procedures. The utilization of soft tooling and inadequate quality assurance procedures will lead to later difficulties and additional costs. The system manager and his or her staff may well investigate the development and utilization of subsystem simulators in cases where the extent of research and development results in a relatively high risk assessment.

Another lesson is that the authority of managers over the work of outside contractors is frequently insufficient to allow the effective discharge of assigned tasks. The past is replete with examples of the upgrading of managers to vice-presidential level, the establishment of autonomous divisions, and other organizational changes in an effort to provide sufficient authority for key managers in the system management process.

Another lesson learned from experience is to question the advisability of imposing, or attempting to impose, management control systems on contractors, subcontractors, or other system participants after the system plan has once been developed and accepted by all participants. The system manager is faced with the same type of difficult decision engineering managers face when the original technical objective has been achieved, but in the achievement, an even better but more time-consuming and therefore more costly way has been seen. Should a better management control system consequently be forced upon participants or will the control system originally developed and approved suffice?

The package approach, whereby the design, development, testing, and manufacture of a system is accomplished by a single contractor, has been debated with some wisdom over a long period of time. It would appear that such a program, negotiated into a single contract, offers an effective instrument for the acquisition of major systems, if the work is accomplished outside the system manager's facilities, with clearly defined objectives and meaningful, measurable incentives.

Experience has also shown the need for knowing what the task entails, if for no other reason than the ability to apply the necessary resources to accomplish the system objective. During the years 1978 and 1979, a number of articles appeared in Dayton, Ohio, newspapers describing in detail problems connected with the nursing-home industry. In one case, an elderly woman patient was reported to have caused her own death "by running hot water into the tub in which she was sitting while the two women employees attending her were out of the bathroom" ([Dayton] *Journal Herald,* September 18, 1979, p. 3). The report continues:

Although the bath water was let out, the state later tested water coming out of the faucet and reported it was 138 degrees.
Investigators said that water even at 120 degrees is awfully hot.
While she was being towel-dried, skin began to peel off her buttocks and heels.
Some Lysol had been put in the bath water, but it was in such a small amount it had no bearing on the burns . . . , the County Coroner said.
It was determined that the original ruling of accidental in the April death of a seventy-four-year-old resident of an East Dayton nursing home will stand.

In another case, reported in the *Dayton Daily News* (September 22, 1979, p. 1 and p. 12), Ohio Health Department officials were moving to try to close a nursing home—a different home than that in the first example—where one patient had been burned and two patients had suffered injuries. The owners and operators of the home "disputed the state findings." They called them groundless and said they stemmed from disgruntled employees.

According to the report, the alleged violations found included the following:

Patients did not receive adequate, kind and considerate care and treatment at all times. A patient suffered second-degree burns from her bath water because the temperature was in excess of requirements.
Nurses' notes did not accurately record how the patient got the burns or how another's leg was fractured. That is a violation because the records and reports required under an Ohio administrative rule were not prepared in a manner approved by the health department.
The home did not maintain the required two-day supply of fresh food, a record of meals served was not on file and meals did not provide minimal nutritional needs as defined by the health department. (A dinner meal consisted of one slice of bologna, two slices of bread, one-fourth cup egg salad with lettuce, a bowl of creamed chicken noodle soup and no fruit, according to the state.)

There was not always a nurse at the home for the minimum sixteen hours per day, between 6 A.M. and midnight.

Patients were not provided with clean pillows and coverings suitable for the winter and some patients had no blanket.

The building was not clean and orderly. Two exit lights were out on the first and second floor. A second-floor handrail was weak, fire extinguishers were in need of service and the exterior porch and steps were in disrepair.

Other violations, according to the state, included improper food storage, a malfunctioning patient-call system, dirty equipment and supplies, improperly stored drugs, leaky plumbing and excessively hot water.

I myself am personally cognizant of a one-day "management development seminar" supposedly catering to the needs of the nursing-home industry. (In the State of Ohio, nursing-home operators must have attended some such "up-dating" program to be eligible for relicensing.) The nursing-home owners, operators, and supervisors were assigned to the same group—for discussion and problem-solving activities. Participants were asked to develop objectives for · their organizations. The nursing-home group developed one objective—"the best care at the lowest price." Efforts to have the group develop measurable objectives were fruitless.

In an exercise designed to help participants determine the resources needed to achieve organizational objectives, the nursing-home group could not, or would not, list the tasks to be accomplished to support the given number of patients in their organizations. There were no job descriptions to determine the loading or expected duties of individual nurses, and there was no way to determine whether sufficient nurses were available on each shift to accomplish the necessary work load. There was no method in use in the nursing homes represented at the seminar to determine the total work load, or to determine the work load of individuals on the staff of the nursing homes. After a recorded five minutes of contemplation of the problem exercise, one outspoken owner objected vociferously to the exercise, and another supervisor said, ". . . we don't have this kind of information."

There are several lessons to be learned from this. A nursing home is a system, albeit small. There are heating, cooling, plumbing needs to be provided; there are menus to prepare, food to be procured, stored, and prepared; there are personal services to be provided the patient; there are supervisory tasks to be performed; and there should be a reasonable profit accruing to the owner to justify his investment. In the two cases cited, there is reason to wonder if the resources necessary to provide the health services were available; if adequate, qualified supervision was available; if sufficient inspections were made and if recommendations for improvement were seriously considered; but there also is reason to wonder if the owners, operators, and supervisors attending the "upgrading" seminar came to learn or merely to be able to show a receipt for payment of such a seminar, regardless of how little participants put into the seminar or got out of it.

MANAGEMENT CONTROL

Provisions for control of the activities called for in the plan to achieve the technical and management objectives of the system manager must be considered in the planning phase. In the control phase, the system manager will be able to measure progress versus time to assure that the system activities are operating within the time and, therefore, the budget or dollar allotment. In controlling intangible activities such as research, development, engineering design, test design, and other intellectual activities not measurable by observation, the system manager will be sorely tested to maintain an awareness of the progress toward goals that such intellectual activities are making.

Control rooms, management by exception or management by review of the areas not on schedule, Gantt charts, individualized program and system charts, the utilization of administrative assistants, computer tie-in and print-out facilities with all dispersed areas of system activities, and the work breakdown system are all viable means of control. None appears quite so effective as the face-to-face progress review by the manager concerned with the scientist or engineer concerned. Together they establish short-range goals by mutual decision. The manager may provide short-term assistance if necessary—perhaps more experienced scientific and engineering talent or greater number of highly skilled engineers and scientists—to overcome obstacles.

Here is an experience of a major corporation which prides itself on its research and engineering capability. In one division of about 2,200 employees, the engineering department consisted of 136 engineers, divided into eight sections with 16 engineers in each section, which was headed by an engineering manager or managing engineer. Each section manager was left to his or her own devices to insure the control of engineering time and effort; he or she was free to use his own managerial philosophy about the control of money and the progress that the engineers under his or her supervision—and thus the programs, projects, or systems on which his or her subordinates were working—were making toward the technical objectives assigned. The control devices utilized by the various managers ranged from (a) a very complicated but very effective use of an administrative assistant, with an engineering degree, to supervise a control room and monitor progress; to (b) the very simple—in any number of ways—device of the section manager knowing in his mind the progress each engineer was making, or in this set of circumstances, not making, as well as the status of each subsystem and of the complete system he or she and his or her personnel were designing for manufacture. It was this latter engineering section that was responsible for the design of the only product or system of the division at this particular time. When the customer canceled the order for the system because of the failure of the system to perform as specified, the entire division was seriously affected. Had the division been an autonomous company, the effect would have been bankruptcy, a cessation of all activities, and the dissolution of the organization. The major corporation in this case could, and did, carry the division until the corporation could again assign work to it.

The point being made is this: The engineering or scientific manager submits a budget of time and dollars to accomplish a predetermined technical objective. The engineering or scientific manager must then establish control points and control devices to assure progress according to plan and the budget he or she submitted. Once control points are established, the relatively mundane task of accumulation of information concerning progress at this particular control point may begin. There is much assistance available to the system manager for the design and operation of information-gathering and information-processing systems. The recognition or/and development of key control points, particularly of intellectual activities, is a lonely task. The work breakdown system offers many advantages for the control of tangible items.

The modern system manager is faced with the control of other areas, deemed intangible until recently, such as attitude and behavior and the relationship of attitude and behavior to financial management and cost control. Research results have demonstrated how a coercive policy by senior management may produce a dramatic increase in cost control and profit on a very short-term basis, with no perceptible change in attitude and behavior (Likert). If, however, the coercive policy is maintained for a period longer than two or three months, the behavior of employees will become such that the cost-savings curve will begin to flatten, and soon, as catastrophe is imminent, the behavior, attitude, and cost savings, or financial management curves, will show a steep decline. The relationships of the financial curve—or trend—the attitude measurement curve, and the behavior measurement curve operate with a time lag. The attitude curve first begins to signal a decline in the early stages, followed by a decline in the behavior measurement curve, then a decline in the financial management curve. When the system manager becomes aware of the catastrophic situation and instills a supportive theory of management, the attitude measurement trend will first show improvement, after employees are convinced the changes in management practices are sincere, desirable, and permanent, followed slowly, and with a considerable lag, by the behavior measurement trend. The improvement time lag is very long. The system manager must develop control devices to alert him to attitude and behavior changes early, so that any downward trend is picked up immediately and a downward momentum prevented.

PREREQUISITES FOR CONTROL

Standards of performance must be developed with which current effort may be compared to allow the system manager to measure the progress being made toward the achievement of the system objectives. Standards of performance may include job descriptions for individuals, objectives for subunits of the organization or system management office divisions, as well as overall system technical and management objectives. Job descriptions are a frequently overlooked tool that can be of major value to the manager. Budgets, developed by subordinate units and subordinate managers in the proposal stage, showing both the time and money necessary for the achievement of unit objectives, are similarly valuable control tools. Admittedly, this discussion may appear an oversimplification, owing to the amount of effort necessary adequately to display this type of information to the system manager and to subordinate managers in timely and visible form. Gantt charts, or some derivation thereof, are widely used to present such information.

Information from selected key points or highly sensitive areas selected as control points may be collected and displayed by some management information system. Program Evaluation and Review (PERT) charts or Critical Path Methods (CPM) may be developed for both overall system objectives and for subsystem objectives. In repetition, the selection of control points is very difficult. Once the control point is selected, there are adequate means to collect the information, compare actual results with expected results, and display the results to the system manager. The system manager is usually satisfied with progress in conformance with the plan, applying his or her energy, expertise, influence, and ability to the control points at variance with the plan. The system manager must be prepared to manage by exception those problem areas where technical problems exist due to the frontiers of science being pushed too far too fast, or due to the behavior problems of individuals or groups because of poor communication, lack of recognition, lack of opportunity for growth, or interface misunderstandings. The manager must be prepared to take remedial action to bring the control point which is out of tolerance back to an acceptable level of performance.

AN APPRAISAL OF THE SYSTEM MANAGEMENT PROCESS

Great strides have been made in the development of management theory. The tools developed by the classical school of thought, which emphasizes the primacy of the functions of management; by the behavioral school of thought, which emphasizes individual and group behavior; and by the scientific management school of thought, which provides mathematical and decision-theory processes; have provided system managers with sufficient theory to develop a workable and successful philosophy of their own. Although each school appears to put primary emphasis on different areas, an approach where the tenets of the classical school are used as a foundation or skeleton for a philosophy, filled out and augmented by the tenets of the behavioral school and the management-science school, offers the system manager a viable and constructive philosophy. Research into management methods continues, and the results of this ongoing effort will benefit managers of the future.

The bureaucratic organization structure has been frequently criticized lately, but it seems that the cause of the deficiencies and the resulting criticism is the people who staff the organization. Individual and group behavior are the subjects of a vast amount of ongoing research. It is certain that the results of this behavioral research will provide additional tools to assist the system manager in his formidable task.

The definition of interfaces and the assignment of responsibilities and accountabilities for such interfaces will do much to eliminate a number of causes of conflict. The interface area, as well as the subject of conflict, offers opportunities for research to discover better ways to reduce tension.

The importance to the system manager of economic, social, political, and general technical environmental conditions has been emphasized. The system manager of the future must develop a keen awareness of environmental trends.

Configuration management procedures and their importance have been discussed, with the admonition that the importance of configuration management will increase as the size, complexity, and number of subsystems in systems increase. Although present procedures appear adequate, change is certain, and there is no doubt but that improved procedures will be developed. The system manager must be prepared to accept change—and even be the catalyst in the process.

Lastly, the importance of planning and control can never be over-emphasized. Again, there are many mnemonic devices to invite attention to planning and control procedures, but as the complexity and ambition of our system technical objectives increase, so will the need for improved planning and control procedures. It thus appears that our incremental step toward improvement of primary management functions will inch forward steadily, as does our technical progress. The system manager can never afford the luxury of satisfaction with the status quo, but must continue the search for improved management procedures as diligently as the pursuit of improved technical objectives.

Robert Katz, in his retrospective commentary on his classical article on the skills of an effective administrator, observes that his original article reporting his research was an attempt to focus attention on demonstrable skills of performance rather than on innate personality. He now believes that human skill can be usefully subdivided into the following categories: (1) leadership ability within the manager's own unit, and (2) skill in inter-group relationships. He observes that in his experience, outstanding capability in one of these areas is frequently accompanied by mediocre performance in the other. Internal intragroup skills are essential in lower and middle management, and intergroup skills become increasingly impor-tant at successively higher levels of management.

Conceptual skills, from the general management point of view, always involve thinking in terms of relative emphases and priorities among con-flicting objectives and criteria, relative tendencies and probabilities rather than certainties, and rough correlations and patterns among elements rather than clear-cut cause-and-effect relationships (Katz, 1974).

Katz now suggests that skill in conceptual perception is an innate ability. He also observes that managers at all levels require some com-petence in each of the three skills. Dealing with the external demands on a manger's unit requires conceptual skill; the limited physical and financial resources available to him or her tax his or her technical skill; and the capabilities and demands of the persons with whom he or she deals make it essential that he or she possess human skill.

This book was written with the hope that it might serve as both an incentive and a point of departure for additional research and discussion of the difficulties and challenges of system management. With an ever--increasing amount of our national resources allocated to the development, design, testing, and utilization of large and complex systems, the system manager needs to be provided with the best tools available and the most perceptive insights that theorists and practitioners can offer.

BIBLIOGRAPHY

Assael, Henry. "Constructive Role of Inter-Organizational Conflict," *Administrative Science Quarterly*, Vol. 14, March 1968.

Athos, Anthony G., and Coffey, Robert E. *Behavior in Organizations: A Multidimensional View.* Englewood Cliffs, New Jersey: Prentice-Hall, 1968.

Baritz, Loren. *The Servants of Power.* Middletown, Connecticut: Wesleyan University, 1960.

Barnard, Chester I. *The Functions of the Executive.* Cambridge: Harvard University Press, 1938.

———. "Functions and Pathology of Status Systems in Formal Organizations" in William Forte Whyte, ed., *Industry and Society,* New York: Greenwood Press, 1946.

Barnet, Richard J., and Muller, Ronald E. *Global Reach.* This section based on article, "World Money Machine," Dayton *Journal Herald,* January 28, 1975, adapted from book.

Bennis, Warren G. *Beyond Bureaucracy.* New York: McGraw-Hill Paperback Ed., 1966a.

———. *Changing Organizations.* New York: McGraw-Hill, 1966b.

———. "Who Sank the Yellow Submarine?" *Psychology Today,* November 1972.

Bertalanffy, Ludwig von. *Kritische Theorie der Formbildung.* Berlin: Borntraeger, 1928.

Blake, Robert R., and Mouton, Jane Srygley. "The Fifth Achievement," *The Journal of Applied Behavioral Science,* Vol. 6, No. 4, 1970, by NTL Institute for Applied Behavioral Science.

———. "Industrial Warfare to Collaboration: A Behavioral Science Approach," a paper prepared as the Korzybski Memorial Address, April 20, 1961.

Blau, Peter M. *Bureaucracy in Modern Society.* New York: Random House, 1956.

Boulding, Kenneth. *Conflict and Defense.* New York: Harper, 1962.

Bryson, Lyman. "Notes on a Theory of Advice," *Political Science Quarterly,* Vol. 66, No. 3, 1951.

Cary, William L. *Politics and the Regulatory Agency.* New York: McGraw-Hill, 1967.

Church, Alexander H. *The Science and Practice of Management.* New York: Engineering Magazine Co., 1914.

Cleland, David I., and King, William R. *Systems, Organizations, Analysis, Management: A Book of Readings.* New York: McGraw-Hill, 1969.

———. *Systems Analysis and Project Management,* 2nd ed. New York: McGraw-Hill, 1975.

Courington, Herbert C., Chief of Configuration Management, General Dynamics/Convair, San Diego, California, "Contracting to Base Lines," *Technical Papers,* Vol. 1, West Coast Configuration Management Symposium, sponsored by the Los Angeles Section of the American Society for Quality Control, copyright 1965 by American Society for Quality Control, Inc. 162 West Wisconsin Avenue, Milwaukee, Wisconsin 53203.

Crozier, Michael. "Human Relations at the Management Level in a Bureaucratic System of Organization," *Human Organization,* Vol. 20, 1965.

Dalton, Melville. *Men Who Manage.* New York: Wiley, 1959.

Davis, Ralph C. *The Fundamentals of Top Management.* New York: Harper, 1951.

Dayton Daily News, Dayton, Ohio, October 10, 1963.

Deutsch, Morton. "Conflicts: Productive and Destructive," *Journal of Social Issues,* 25 (1969), Kurt Lewin Memorial Address given at meetings of the American Psychological Association, September 1, 1968, in San Francisco.

Dietle, Joseph F., Supervisor, Configuration Accounting/Verification Unit, Minuteman Division, Autonetics Division of North American Aviation, Inc. (now Rockwell International Corp.), "Minuteman Configuration Accounting," in *Technical Papers,* Vol. 1, West Coast Configuration Management Symposium, sponsored by the Los Angeles Section of the American Society for Quality Control, copyright 1965 by American Society for Quality Control, Inc., 161 West Wisconsin Avenue, Milwaukee, Wisconsin 53203.

Dubin, Robert, in Tannenbaum, Robert; Weschler, Irving R.; and Massarik, Fred, *Leadership and Organization: A Behavioral Science Approach.* New York: McGraw-Hill, 1961.

Dutton, John M., and Walton, Richard E. "Interdepartmental Conflict and Cooperation: Two Contrasting Studies," *Human Organization,* Vol. 25, 1966.

Eaglesfield, Charles C. "The Development in the Art of Generating Coherent Wave Forms, The Nature of Laser Light," *A Guide to the Laser,* ed. David Fishlock. London: MacDonald, 1967.

Evan, William Martin, "Conflict and Performance in R & D Organizations," *Industrial Management Review,* Vol. 7, No. 1, Fall 1965, pp. 37-46.

Fayol, Henri. *Industrial and General Administration.* Geneva: International Management Institute, 1930.

Galbraith, John K. *The Great Crash.* Boston: Houghton Mifflin, 1955.

Gallese, Liz Roman. "The Soothsayers," *Wall Street Journal,* March 31, 1975.

Groves, Leslie R. *Now it Can Be Told–The Story of the Manhattan Project.* New York: Harper, 1962.

Gutmann, Peter M., ed. *Economic Growth.* Englewood Cliffs, New Jersey, Prentice-Hall, 1965.

Hall, Richard H. "The Concept of Bureaucracy: An Empirical Assessment," *American Journal of Sociology,* Vol. 69, 1963.

Heider, Fritz. "Social Perception and Phenomenal Causality," *Psychological Review,* Vol. 51, 1944.

Helmer, Olaf, and Gordon, Theodore. "Generation of Internally Consistent Scenarios Through the Study of Cross-Impact." Paper presented at the Industrial Management Center, Austin, Texas, January 27-30, 1969.

Kahn, Herman. *The Future of the Corporation.* New York: Mason and Lipscomb, 1974.

———, and Bruce-Briggs, Barry. *Things to Come.* New York: Macmillan, 1972.

Kahn, Robert L., et al. *Studies in Organizational Stress.* New York: Wiley, 1964.

Katz, Daniel. "Approaches to Managing Conflict," in Robert L. Kahn and Kenneth Boulding, eds., *Power and Conflict in Organizations.* New York: Basic Books, 1964.

Katz, Robert L. "Skills of an Effective Administrator," *Harvard Business Review,*

January-February 1955 issue, reprinted in *Harvard Business Review,* with retrospective commentary, September-October 1974.

Kohlmeier, Louis M., Jr. *The Regulators.* New York: Harper and Row, 1969.

Koontz, Harold. "The Management Theory Jungle," *Journal of the Academy of Management,* Vol. 4, No. 3, December 1961.

———, and O'Donnell, Cyril. *Principles of Management,* 3d. ed. New York: McGraw-Hill, 1964.

Kuznets, Simon S. *Secular Movements in Production and Prices.* Cambridge, Massachusetts: Riverside Press, 1930.

Lanford, Horace W. *An Analysis of Coordinative Methods in Air Force Systems Management.* Aeronautical Systems Division, Air Force Systems Command, Wright-Patterson AFB, Dayton, Ohio, 1965.

———. *Technological Forecasting Methodologies: A Synthesis.* New York: American Management Association, 1972.

Lawrence, Paul R., and Lorsch, Jay W. *Organization and Environment.* Boston: Division of Research, Graduate School of Business Administration, Harvard University, 1967, and "Differentiation and Integration in Complex Organizations," *Administrative Science Quarterly,* Vol. 12, 1967.

Lewin, Kurt. *Resolving Social Conflict.* New York: Harper, 1958.

Likert, Rensis, quoted by Saul Gellerman in "Motivation in Perspective," a training film, BNA Communications, Inc., Rockville, Maryland.

Litwak, Eugene. "Models of Bureaucracy Which Permit Conflict," *American Journal of Sociology,* Vol. 67, 1961.

Loughry, Donald C. "What Makes a Good Interface?" *IEEE Spectrum,* November 1974.

McCarthy, Robert M., Manager, Master Scheduling, Lockheed Space Systems Division, Sunnyvale, California, in "Configuration Management, Lockheed Space Systems Division," p. 99, *Technical Papers,* Vol. 1, West Coast Configuration Management Symposium, sponsored by the Los Angeles Section of the American Society for Quality Control, held at the Disneyland Hotel in Anaheim, California, August 19 and 20, 1965, copyright 1965 by American Society for Quality Control, Inc., 161 West Wisconsin Avenue, Milwaukee, Wisconsin 53203.

McDonough, Adrian M. *Information Economics and Management Systems.* New York: McGraw-Hill, 1963.

McGregor, Douglas. *Antioch Notes,* Vol. 31, No. 9, May 1, 1954.

MacNulty, Christine Ralph. "The Political Scenario," paper presented at an American Management Associations conference on Technological Forecasting, New York, May 1975.

March, James G., and Simon, Herbert A. *Organizations.* New York: Wiley, 1958.

Meadows, Donella H., et al. *The Limits to Growth.* New York: Universe Books, 1972.

Mee, John F. *Management Thought in a Dynamic Economy.* New York: New York University Press, 1963.

Miles, Robert H., and Randolph, W. Alan. *The Organization Game* (Participants' Manual). Santa Monica, California: Goodyear Publishing Company, 1979.

Miller, Gerald R. *Conflict Resolution Through Communication.* New York: Harper and Row, 1973.

Moore, Wilbert E. *Industrial Relations and the Social Order,* 2nd edition, New York: Arno Press, 1951.

Mulder, Mauk, and Wilke, Henk. "Participation and Power Equalization," *Organizational Behavior and Human Performance,* Vol. 5, No. 5, September 1970.

Oxford Universal Dictionary. London: Oxford University Press, 1975.

Pearl, Raymond. *Studies in Human Biology.* Baltimore: Williams and Wilkins Co., 1924.

Peck, Merton J., and Scherer, Frederic M. *The Weapons Acquisition Process.* Boston: Harvard Business School, 1962.

Pondy, Louis R. "Organizational Conflict: Concepts and Models," *Administrative Science Quarterly,* Vol. 12, 1967.

Production. "News Digest," February 1975.

Reckmeyer, William J. "Weapon System Management." Ph.D. dissertation, Ohio State University, 1958.

Samaras, Thomas T., and Czerwinski, Frank L. *Fundamentals of Configuration Management.* New York: Wiley Interscience, 1971.

Schmidt, Warren H. "Conflict, a Powerful Process for (Good or Bad) Change," *Management Review,* AMACOM, New York, Vol. 63, No. 12, December 1974.

Scott, William G., and Mitchell, Terence R. *Organizational Theory: A Structural and Behavioral Analysis.* Homewood, Illinois: Richard D. Irwin, 1972.

Seiler, John A. "Diagnosing Interdepartmental Conflict," *Harvard Business Review,* Vol. 41, September–October 1963.

Shomper, Richard F., and Phillips, Victor F., Jr. *Management in Bureaucracy,* and AMA Management briefing, AMACOM, 1973, New York.

Simon, Herbert A. *Administrative Behavior.* New York: Macmillan, 1957.

Smith, Claggett G. "A Comparative Analysis of Some Conditions and Consequences of Intra-Organizational Conflict," *Administrative Science Quarterly,* Vol. 10, March 1966.

Syracuse University Research Corporation, *The United States and the World in the 1985 Era,* Clearinghouse Document AD 613 527, Defense Documentation Center, Defense Supply Agency, March 1964.

Tannenbaum, Arnold S. "Control Structure and Union Functions," *American Journal of Sociology,* Vol. 61, 1956.

Tannenbaum, Robert, and Weschler, Irving R., and Massarik, Fred. *Leadership and Organization: A Behavioral Science Approach.* New York: McGraw-Hill, 1961.

Thibant, John W., and Kelley, Harold H. *The Social Psychology of Groups.* New York: Wiley, 1959.

Thompson, James D. "Organizational Management of Conflict," *Administrative Science Quarterly,* Vol. 4, 1959–60.

Thompson, Victor A. "Hierarchy, Specialization, and Organizational Conflict," *Administrative Science Quarterly,* Vol. 5, 1961.

Toffler, Alvin. *Future Shock.* New York: Bantam Books, 1970.

Wall Street Journal, May 15, 1975.

Walton, Richard E. "Theory of Conflict in Lateral Organizational Relationships," Institute Paper No. 85. Lafayette, Ind.: Purdue University, November 1964.

———, and Dutton, John M. "The Management of Interdepartmental Conflict: A Model and Review," *Administrative Science Quarterly,* Vol. 14, 1969.

———, and Fitch, H. Gordon. "A Study of Conflict in the Process, Structure, and Attitudes of Lateral Relationships," Institute Paper No. 93. Lafayette, Ind.: Purdue University, November 1964.

Walton, Richard E., and McKersie, Robert B. *A Behavioral Theory of Labor Negotiations.* New York: McGraw-Hill, 1965.

Wren, Daniel A. *The Evolution of Management Thought.* New York: Ronald Press, 1972.

Zald, Mayer N. "Power Balance and Staff Conflict in Correctional Institutions," *Administrative Science Quarterly,* Vol. 7, 1964.

INDEX